THE ESSENTIAL SEX EDUCATION BOOK FOR PARENTS

THE ESSENTIAL
SEX EDUCATION
BOOK FOR PARENTS

Guided Conversations
to Have with Your Tweens and Teens

DANIEL RICE

ROCKRIDGE
PRESS

For Mom and Dan, whose lessons on love, empathy, and inclusivity have shaped my life view and are reflected in these pages

Interior and Cover Designer: Michael Cook
Art Producer: Sara Feinstein
Editor: Brian Sweeting
Production Editor: Sigi Nacson
Production Manager: Holly Hayworth

Author photo: Nicole Seoage

Paperback ISBN: 978-1-63807-422-9 | eBook ISBN: 978-1-63807-831-9
R0

Contents

Introduction   *vi*

About the Guided Conversations in This Book   *ix*

Part 1: The Basics   *1*

Chapter 1   Understanding Your Child's
Sexual Development   *2*

Chapter 2   Exploring the "Why?" and "How?"   *17*

Part 2: The Conversations   *29*

Chapter 3   Growing Up   *30*

Chapter 4   Nurturing Relationships to Thrive   *54*

Chapter 5   Sex: The Behaviors and the
Societal Constructs   *72*

Chapter 6   Consent and Safer Sex   *90*

Chapter 7   The Internet, Social Media,
and Pornography   *112*

A Final Word   *121*

Resources   *122*

References   *124*

Index   *130*

Introduction

Thank you for choosing *The Essential Sex Education Book for Parents* as a resource for guiding your conversations about sexuality with your tweens and teens. Many possible circumstances may have drawn you to this book. Maybe you're seeking advice on how to talk about a particular topic. Perhaps your child is starting puberty, and you want to know how to talk to them about the changes they will experience. Or maybe you're just looking for some guidance from a professional in the sex education field. Regardless of the reason, I welcome all parents who recognize the importance of learning about sexuality and want to convey their values and beliefs related to the topic, but just don't know where to begin. Our combined expertise—mine as a sex educator, and yours as the parent or caregiver of your child—will provide the resources necessary to have these important conversations.

Let's begin with some basic principles I'm bringing to this book:

+ The word *sexuality* is used in this book to refer to the model of holistic sexuality developed in 1981 by Dr. Dennis Dailey, which encompasses sexual and reproductive health, sexual identity, intimacy, sensuality, and sexualization.

+ When a person is born, the doctor will usually announce their sex based on their genitalia. If a person has a vulva, they are assigned female at birth (AFAB). If they have a penis, they are assigned male at birth (AMAB). It is important to discern that sex and gender are not the same thing. While sex is often assigned based on our genitals, our gender is our internal sense of being male, female, nonbinary, or any number of other identities. This book celebrates all identities as being more than worthy of love and happiness.

- Communicating about sexuality is often referred to as "the talk." However, it is impossible to have one conversation that will meet the needs of your children at every point of their development. Talking about sexuality must be a lifelong conversation—that's why this book includes 70 different guided conversations.
- While the focus of this book is on tweens and teens, it's important to note that conversations about sexuality can, and should, start during very early childhood.
- Finally, sexuality should be addressed from a positive perspective. If we're not honest with young people about the positive aspects of sexuality, such as self- and mutual pleasure, we are contributing to the narrative of shame and stigma. This book reflects this value.

For some parents and caregivers, having these conversations can be quite overwhelming and uncomfortable. Over my 20-year career, I have talked with parents from various backgrounds and provided guidance around how to talk about sexuality. One of the greatest concerns I hear is this: "If I talk to my child about sex, won't they be curious and want to go out and try it?" or "Won't they think I approve of them having sex?" Research shows that when young people have the full range of information, skills, and facts they need related to sexuality, they will make the best decisions for themselves, often leading them to delay their first sexual experience. Many parents and caregivers also believe that sex education is being taught in school, so they don't need to talk with their children about the topic. Although some states require sex education in schools, accountability mechanisms that ensure honest, accurate sex education is being implemented are rarely in place, so the accuracy and quality of the information varies from classroom to classroom.

The fact is, parents and caregivers are the primary sex educators of the young people in their lives. This is why it was so important to me to write this book. My friends often send me messages seeking guidance around questions their children have asked about sexuality, and they joke about keeping me on retainer for professional support. My hope is that after reading this book, parents and caregivers will feel empowered to have honest, sex-positive conversations with the young people in their lives. Part 1 provides a very basic overview of sexual development and how to talk with children about sexuality. This information is foundational to part 2, which includes conversations organized by topic area, but not necessarily in chronological order.

About the Guided Conversations in This Book

The purpose of the guided conversations is to provide parents and caregivers with a starting point for having critical conversations about sexuality with their children. It would be both impossible and ineffective to try to provide an exact script for these conversations. Every child and family is different, so every conversation must be tailored to their individual needs. Keep in mind that the age ranges indicated in each conversation should be considered guidance—this is where your expertise in your child's personal development becomes important. If your child is neuroatypical, it's still important to have these conversations, but they may occur at different ages than those noted, or it may be helpful to use adjusted language or have conversations in a different environment.

The prompts are intended to provide a range of important topics parents and caregivers have expressed a desire to discuss, along with basic information on each one. Some of the topics included are often missing from the typical sex education classroom, so they will fill in content gaps even if your child is receiving high-quality sex education. Each conversation will provide specific questions, prompts, and sample language to facilitate a meaningful discussion. Feel free to flip to any page in the guided conversation section that calls to you. This book is not meant to be approached chronologically since the structure of the conversations isn't hierarchical. For example, you may want to start reading some of the first topics in chapter 6 in tandem with the other chapters, because consent conversations should be woven into all the guided conversations. All topics will work for parents and any child, but some are specific to children based on whether they are AFAB or AMAB.

The Basics

Part 1 provides the foundational information necessary to have successful conversations with the young people in your life. It begins with a primer on adolescent sexual development and general guidelines for talking with your child about sexuality. In addition to the physical changes of puberty, chapter 1 covers cognitive, emotional, and social changes—including the development of gender and sexual identities—and the role of modern technology in adolescent development. Chapter 2 provides a brief look at sex education in schools, discusses why sex-positive conversations are important, and provides tips for how to initiate sexuality conversations with the young people you care for.

Understanding Your Child's Sexual Development

Chapter 1 is intended to provide information that is foundational to having the conversations in part 2 of this book. It begins with a basic overview, then guides you through the physical, cognitive, and emotional changes that occur during puberty and adolescence. As you move through this chapter, keep in mind that these changes are not happening in a linear progression as they are written. Many changes often overlap, and each change impacts the others—those that have already happened and those yet to come. Understanding your child's sexual development will help you determine when they might be ready for the conversations in part 2 and why they might respond in different ways.

A Primer on Sexual Development

We are all sexual beings from the time we are born. Our sexuality is a part of who we are as human beings, and not acknowledging a young person's sexuality means missing a part of who they are as an individual. If you've thought about sexual development in a holistic way, you may have already realized that it's not just about the physical changes our bodies go through during puberty. Sexual development also includes the social and emotional changes we experience—changes that inform how we develop relationships with ourselves and others.

It's important to remember that all children do not begin puberty at the same time or develop at the same rate. For young people who may be questioning their gender identity, puberty might be particularly fraught with anxiety because the parts of their body they identify with the least will begin to develop and become more prominent. I'll talk more about this later in the chapter. Let's begin by exploring some of the basics of puberty and adolescence. I'll then outline some of the physical changes that occur in people of all genders before breaking down the changes unique to people assigned female at birth (AFAB) and assigned male at birth (AMAB)—terms that I'll use throughout the book.

The Onset of Puberty and Universal Physical Changes

Puberty is the period when the body starts to physically change from a child to an adult. The changes of puberty begin at different times and typically take around five to seven years to complete. People AFAB will often begin the changes of puberty at an earlier age than people AMAB. *Adolescence* is the period that begins with the onset of puberty, or around age 10, but continues past the completion of physical changes. Cognitive, emotional, and social changes continue to occur until adolescence concludes, typically until the early 20s. As we begin to explore the changes of puberty, it is important to remember that, as humans, we are biologically more alike than we are different. This means many of the physical changes of puberty will occur in people of all sexes.

When a child is between 8 and 10 years of age, the pituitary gland, a pea-sized gland in the brain, begins to release hormones that will trigger the onset of puberty. As this occurs, the first physical signs of the changes of puberty will be present. Universally, the body begins to grow faster and may experience rapid growth spurts, so adolescents need more sleep at this stage than at any other point in their lives. Due to the increase of hormones in the body, sweat glands will begin to produce more sweat and bacteria that may produce body odor. All these changing hormones in the body may also result in the development of acne. Cleaning the body with warm soap and water will help wash away the bacteria and excess oils that can cause body odor and acne. People of all genders will also begin to develop hair under their arms and around their genitals.

Physical Changes in People AFAB

For people AFAB, puberty typically begins between the ages of 8 and 13. The development of breast buds (swelling tissue under the nipples) is the first physical sign of the onset of puberty. The breasts may feel tender or sore and may develop at different speeds, and the breast tissue may feel lumpy. This is all perfectly normal. People AFAB begin to develop pubic hair shortly after the development of the breasts. As your child gets older and compares their body to others', they may have questions about shaving, waxing, or grooming their leg, underarm and/or pubic hair. This is a personal choice, but there is no biological need to remove or trim any of these areas of hair.

About two years after the start of breast development, between the ages of 10 and 16, people AFAB will typically experience their first menses, commonly referred to as their "period." Talking with your child about menstruation before it begins can help minimize any anxiety they may have when it happens. The typical menstrual cycle is about 28 days, though it can be longer or shorter for some people and is often very irregular in frequency for young people. When menstruation first starts, it's common for the body to take some time to develop a regular cycle, so always being prepared with a tampon, pad, or menstrual cup is a good idea. Diet and exercise routines can also impact the regularity of a person's cycle. Taking a hot bath, applying a heating pad, or taking over-the-counter pain relievers can reduce pain from cramping. Other physical changes of puberty include getting taller, the onset of daily discharge from the vagina, and the widening of the hips to allow for carrying and birthing children if the individual chooses to.

Physical Changes in People AMAB

For people AMAB, puberty typically begins between the ages of 9 and 14. The enlargement of the testicles and scrotum is the first physical sign of the onset of puberty. The skin of the scrotum becomes darker in color and hangs lower from the body. Hair follicles also develop on the scrotum and appear as little bumps. For most people AMAB, one testicle will usually hang lower than the other. About one year later, the penis will also begin to grow in size and length. While testosterone is the dominant hormone in people AMAB, they also have estrogen in their bodies, just as people AFAB also have small amounts of testosterone in their bodies. For this reason, some people AMAB may also show signs of breast development, but this will usually resolve as they grow. Pubic hair typically appears around the age of 13. Similar to people AFAB, shaving or grooming facial hair, body hair, or pubic hair for people AMAB is a personal choice, and there is no biological need to remove or trim it.

UNDERSTANDING GENDER IDENTITY AND EXPRESSION

All people have a gender identity, which is our inner understanding of our gender as a woman, a man, nonbinary, transgender, or another identity. When a person's gender identity matches their sex assigned at birth, the person is considered cisgender. When a person's gender identity does not match their sex assigned at birth, they may identify as gender non-conforming, non-binary, or transgender.

Sex assigned at birth is the term used to describe the label a person is given by a medical professional when they are born, based on their external genitals. People with a vulva are typically given the label *female*, while people with a penis are typically labeled *male*. Developmentally, most people have a sense of their gender identity between the ages of two and three. While they may not have the language to identify as cisgender, gender non-conforming, or transgender, a young person can easily tell you if they identify as a boy, a girl, or neither one. Other identities include nonbinary (one who cannot be defined within the margins of the male/female gender binary), genderqueer (one who does not subscribe to the expected gender norms set forth by society), gender fluid (one who does not have a fixed identity), and many more.

Gender expression is how someone externally expresses their gender—it may be through their choice of clothing, haircut, makeup, jewelry, or through other choices. While *gender expression* is a choice on behalf of each individual, our *gender identity* is not something we choose. If your child is questioning their gender identity or identifies as transgender, you may want to consider, with your child's pediatrician, the option of hormone-blocking therapies, which can slow down the physical changes of puberty. A list of resources is available at the end of this book for parents whose children are questioning or exploring their gender identity and/or contemplating a transition.

Around the age of 14, some people AMAB may experience the release of semen while they are sleeping, called "nocturnal emissions," or wet dreams. Talking with your child about wet dreams before they happen can help reduce the shame and embarrassment they may feel if they mistakenly think that they have wet the bed. Frequent and spontaneous erections are another common experience for people AMAB during puberty. Around the age of 15, or two years after the development of pubic hair, they may begin to develop facial hair and hair under their arms. Other changes that occur during puberty include the deepening of the voice and a growth spurt that changes the proportion of their body, with shoulders getting broader and the muscle mass continuing to fill out.

Cognitive and Emotional Development

In addition to the many physical changes that occur during puberty, important cognitive and emotional changes also begin during this time and continue throughout adolescence. *Cognitive development* refers to the physical changes of the brain and the way it processes information. Understanding the basics of cognitive development will be a great foundation as you talk with your child. The use of drugs and/or alcohol during adolescence can have an adverse effect on how the brain develops. Alcohol and marijuana use is associated with poorer cognitive functioning on tests of verbal and working memory, attention, cognitive control, and overall IQ. Emotional development involves learning what feelings and emotions are, understanding how and why they occur, recognizing one's own feelings and those of others, and developing ways to manage those feelings. Emotional changes, such as mood swings, increased desire for independence, and the development of romantic feelings are important developmental tasks. Trauma from adverse childhood experiences, such as the death or incarceration of a parent, can also have an impact on an individual's emotional development. Ultimately, tweens' and teens' emotional experiences can greatly inform their personal, professional, and romantic relationships well into the future.

Concrete versus Abstract Thinking

Children are concrete thinkers. This means they experience the world in facts, as tangible objects, and in very literal terms. They see things as black or white, good or bad. As they grow older, they develop the capacity for abstract thinking. Abstract thinking is the ability to consider a concept that is not tied to a physical object, such as intimacy or freedom, and make generalizations. Abstract thinking skills typically develop between the ages of 12 and 18. If a child has not developed abstract thinking skills, it can be difficult to have conversations concerning planning for the distant future because they may not be able to understand such a concept. They may understand the distant future as tomorrow or next week, but not 10 years from now. Trying to have conversations about a future relationship or partner, or the impact drugs and alcohol can have on their body as they get older, will not be effective with concrete thinkers. Some of the discussion prompts in part 2 are better suited to concrete thinkers, and others will require your child to have some ability to think abstractly.

The Prefrontal Cortex

The prefrontal cortex (PFC) is the part of the brain just behind the forehead. It's responsible for cognitive control and thereby influences attention, impulse inhibition, prospective memory, and cognitive flexibility. It's also responsible for executive functions, such as planning, working memory, flexibility, and processing speed. Unfortunately, the PFC is the last part of the brain to fully develop—usually around age 25. This means the part of the brain responsible for decision-making and impulse control is not fully developed until *after* the teenage years. The lack of impulse control, combined with peer pressure and the belief that everyone is watching them, is the reason adolescents are more likely to take greater risks and sometimes have an "It can never happen to me" mentality. This is why it is important to develop, practice, and model the skills necessary to assess risk in different situations. Developing a plan that gives your child a way out of an uncomfortable or dangerous situation can be a great strategy. For example, they may text you a word or phrase that is your cue to call them and tell them that they need to come home or that you are coming to pick them up.

Mood Swings

Emotional ups and downs, commonly referred to as "mood swings," are typical during puberty and are caused by increased hormones, such as estrogen and testosterone, being introduced into the body. Your child may go through a wide variety of emotions in a short period and for no apparent reason. As strange as this behavior may seem to you, it probably seems equally strange to them. When these changes in mood occur, they present an opportunity for you to help your child identify and verbalize how they are feeling.

If they have trouble identifying the emotion, ask them to select an emoji from your messaging platform that looks like how they feel and discuss what the emoji represents. This can be helpful in putting a name to the emotion. If your child is feeling great levels of sadness or hopelessness for an extended period (more than a week or two), they may be suffering from depression, and additional help may be warranted.

The same is true if your child is experiencing anxiety for prolonged periods. If your child ever mentions hurting themself or threatens to do so, this should always be taken seriously, and professional help should be contacted (see the Resources section in the back of this book).

Striving for Independence

As young people move along their passage to adulthood, they become less dependent on their parents and start to take on more personal responsibility. As you and your child negotiate new boundaries that allow for greater independence, you may experience more arguments. This is completely normal. All the skills they're learning regarding communication, empathy, decision-making, and problem-solving are moving them toward a greater sense of autonomy and self-efficacy.

It's important to allow your child to make mistakes as they grow. Developing critical thinking skills as they determine how to correct their mistakes, and learning how to handle failure and rejection will help build their self-esteem. They must also learn to take responsibility and be held accountable for the impacts of their actions, regardless of their intent. Achieving independence doesn't mean your child no longer needs you. They need to know they can come to you if they are in danger or need help. You may want to be there to cheer them on, provide support, and remind them of your love. Ultimately, these experiences will result in your tween or teen developing a stronger sense of who they are as an individual.

Romantic Feelings

During puberty, young people—including individuals with differing physical and cognitive abilities—may start to develop romantic feelings for other people. I'm specifically calling

THE IMPACT OF MODERN TECHNOLOGY

Cell phones, video messaging, and social media are just some examples of technology that has helped make communication and accessibility easier for families. These same technologies have also allowed young people to access pornography more easily and engage in behaviors such as *sexting* (the trading of nude or partially nude pictures with others). For tweens and teens, using modern technology comes with both pros and cons.

We know how technology can keep us connected to family, friends, and loved ones when we're not able to be with them physically. However, one of the challenges concerning modern technology, particularly texting and other chat platforms, is that we can't hear the tone of someone's voice, so often we have to speculate about the feelings underlying their words.

Access to technology has also increased access to pornography. Watching videos created for adult entertainment may lead young people to develop unrealistic expectations of how their bodies and sexual relationships should look. On the positive side, social media has provided an outlet for young people to explore different aspects of their identities in a relatively safe environment. Technology has allowed lesbian, gay, bisexual, transgender, queer, and other (LGBTQ+) youth to connect with other young people who are exploring their sexual and gender identities, reducing the feelings of isolation that previous generations may have felt.

Ultimately, use of technology in teen relationships has become ubiquitous. We can't fully understand teen relationships without also understanding the role technology plays in their lives. Apps that track your period, provide reminders about contraception use, and even help provide a line of defense against sexual violence have all made positive contributions to aspects of sexuality. Finding the right balance and providing guidance and boundaries for your child can help minimize the risks.

attention to this community because their sexual feelings and desires are often overlooked, even though they are just as deserving of loving romantic relationships as anyone else. Throughout my career, I've heard adults refer to young people's feelings as "puppy love" and other terms that minimize their emotions. It's important to recognize that these feelings are real and should not be minimized in this way. Adolescent relationships are quite formative because they provide opportunities for individuals to develop skills involving communication, negotiation, and compromise; to explore their own identity; and to feel a greater sense of autonomy, intimacy, and pleasure.

Unfortunately, rejection and the ending of relationships are also part of developing romantic feelings. These situations are important for the growth and development of a young person's sense of resilience and self-respect. Keep in mind that some people do not experience romantic feelings; these people may identify as being "asexual." If your child identifies as asexual, you can support their feelings without attempting to convince them that they should have romantic feelings.

Social Development

Social development is another important task of becoming an adult. The interactions young people have early on with their family and friends become a model for how they will interact with others in adulthood. Communication skills, respect, empathy, decision-making skills, setting goals and boundaries, and other important skills are all developed through our social interactions with others. Mass media is also a factor in young people's social development. This includes messages broadcast in movies, in music, on TV, in magazines, on billboards, and through other sources. For example, visibility or lack of visibility when it comes to differing identities and abilities can affirm or exclude young people with marginalized identities. It's important to monitor and discuss the messages your child is receiving from these outlets so they're not left to interpret the messages on their own. Some of the changes you may notice during adolescence may include, but are not limited to, a growing desire for privacy; developing self-esteem and body image; exploration of values and beliefs; development of sexual identity; and susceptibility to increased influence of their peers. These changes are all important to helping your child discover who they will be and how they will interact with others as an adult. Let's take a closer look at each of these changes.

A Growing Desire for Privacy

As your child's body begins to change during puberty, they will exhibit a growing desire for more privacy. You may feel as if your child is pushing you away or shutting you out, but don't take it personally—they're likely just feeling self-conscious about the physical changes happening to their body. During this time, your child may begin to experiment with masturbation for pleasure, so knocking before entering a room with a closed door is a good idea and models good boundaries.

An increasing desire for privacy also may occur during appointments with your child's pediatrician. It's important to allow your child to have time with the doctor without you in the room so they can ask the doctor questions and have their concerns addressed in private. This will contribute to your child's evolving sense of autonomy and health literacy.

Your child also will likely show an increased desire for privacy in terms of their friendships. Coming to an agreement with your child about how you'll balance privacy and safety can help build trust between you. For example, knowing your child's password on digital devices but agreeing to use it only if you are concerned about their behavior or well-being can be a great way to balance privacy with safety.

Self-Esteem and Body Image

Self-esteem has to do with an individual's sense of self-worth and how valuable they think they are to others. Young people also may base their self-esteem on, for example, academic achievements or how successful they are in a sport or activity they are passionate about. Studies have shown a correlation between self-esteem and the onset of sexual behavior, but the results may not be what you think: Research tells us that people AFAB with higher self-esteem are three times less likely to have sex, while people AMAB who have higher self-esteem are two and a half times more likely to initiate sex.

Body image refers to how a person physically sees themself. As young people begin to experience the physical changes of puberty, they will become more aware of their body and start to compare their body with those of their peers. For this reason, body image often becomes tied to self-esteem during puberty. As a result, eating disorders or obsessive gym routines may begin around this time. If you notice changes in your child's eating or exercising habits, it's important to discuss and monitor their behaviors to ensure that they do not become unhealthy.

Values and Beliefs

One of the tasks of puberty is to begin to develop one's own system of values and beliefs. Although you may have been very clear in articulating your own values, beliefs, and expectations with your children, testing those values and beliefs is perfectly normal. Most people don't grow up with the exact same sets of values and beliefs their parents did. Our values and beliefs change throughout our lives and remain fluid, even in adulthood. Exploring your child's values in a nonjudgmental way and providing additional information, including a range of options regarding certain beliefs, will empower them to think critically about the values and beliefs they are developing. This can be achieved by using the SOW method:

Some people believe ...,
Other people believe ..., and
We (your family) believe ...

The SOW method allows you to present a range of values and beliefs while also expressing the beliefs of your family. Once you've done so, give your child an opportunity to share their beliefs and values on the topic. It is important to present the "Some people ..." and "Other people ..." statements in an inclusive, nonjudgmental manner. In divorced, foster, or other configurations of families, the "We" statement may also need to be modified to reflect the range of values that might exist there. If you push back on any values or beliefs your child holds, do so in a calm and respectful manner so the lines of communication remain open for future conversations except in cases where their beliefs may be harmful to others. In these cases, it is important to be firm with your position.

Sexual Identity

As young people begin to experience romantic feelings, they will start to explore their sexual identity. When some people think of sexual identity (what we call ourselves in connection to our sexual orientation), they automatically think of identities like lesbian, gay, or bisexual individuals, but everyone has a sexual identity—including those who identify as heterosexual, or straight. Sexual orientation is defined by the gender(s) of those we are physically, emotionally, and sexually/romantically attracted to. For example, a person who is physically, emotionally, and sexually attracted to someone of another gender may identify as heterosexual, and a person who is physically, emotionally, and sexually attracted to someone of the same gender may identify as gay or lesbian. It is important to note that a person's identity does not always match their orientation. For example, a person's orientation may be lesbian, but they may identify as straight for a host of reasons.

As a parent, the most important thing you can do for your child, as it relates to this process, is to love and support them. If you believe your child might be questioning their sexual identity, it's best to show your support for them without directly asking them what their identity is. They need to know there's no rush to put a label on their feelings, and they should feel free to do so if/when they're ready.

Increased Influence of Peers

The relationships and opinions of your child's peers will begin to take on greater importance to them during puberty. As they are exploring their own identity, they may begin to grow apart from childhood friends and transition into new social groups. They may also experiment with different hair and clothing styles to fit in with their new peers. During this time, peer pressure may also become a major factor in your child's life. The increased influence of peers is not limited to in-person relationships, but extends online, including people and influencers they have never met. If many of their peers have a presence on social media and are gathering there, your child may request permission to have a presence in these virtual social circles as well.

Social acceptance in their peer groups will become critically important. As your child becomes involved in different social groups, you'll want to get to know the friends they're engaging with the most. Consider allowing your child to have their friends over or to host a social gathering while you're at home. You can attend school events like athletic games, plays, and concerts and see them and their peers in action.

Exploring the "Why?" and "How?"

Chapter 2 provides basic, overarching information on why talking about sexuality with young people is essential and suggestions for how to talk with your child(ren) about sexuality. I'll provide some models typically used in the sex education classroom that have been modified to better meet the needs of a diverse range of families. These models can be applied to the conversations in part 2 to mitigate some of the challenges many parents may experience—like when and how to begin these important talks. There's no single way to have a conversation about sexuality, so as you explore the content, focus on the models and approaches you believe will work best for you.

The Importance of Sex-Positive Talks

My first lesson on sexuality was in sixth grade. We watched a video about the physical changes we would experience during puberty, and then the teacher said, "I'm not here to tell you how to do it (have sex), but if you have any other questions, I will answer them." My second lesson was in my eighth-grade health class, where we were shown images of genitals with sexually transmitted infections (STIs). The final lesson was in ninth-grade biology. Here we watched a video of a person giving birth. The three messages I took from these experiences were: I should not talk about sex; if I have sex, I will get a disease; and if I have sex, my partner will get pregnant (and giving birth is terrifying).

As you can see, just because your child is getting information about sexuality doesn't mean they are receiving positive messages. Some sexual education approaches can be incomplete and shrouded in shame, stigma, and fear. Then, when young people become adults, they are suddenly expected to have healthy sexual relationships and celebrate pregnancy and childbirth. The disconnect here is huge.

Sex positivity is about feeling liberated from shame, stigma, and fear about our bodies, our sexual health, and our sexual experiences. This positivity can't just be turned on like a light switch at adulthood. As a parent, you can talk to your child about sexuality from a positive perspective. It won't make your child want to go out and have sex. If and when they do choose to have sex, do you want them to feel ashamed or embarrassed about it, or feel good knowing they had the information they needed to make it a safer, more pleasurable experience?

If you're worried that your child will become pregnant or get an STI, consider that in cultures that promote positive attitudes toward sex, teens initiate sex at later ages, and have lower pregnancy and STI rates. Sex-positive conversations will likely result in your child developing a healthier attitude about their sexuality and having safer, more pleasurable, shame- and guilt-free sexual experiences.

What Children Don't Learn in School

Laws guiding what young people learn in school vary from state to state. At the time of this publication, only 30 states require sex education to be part of the curriculum, and what can and cannot be included varies among those states. For example, only 11 states require sex education to be inclusive of LGBTQ+, and six states require only negative information to be provided on LGBTQ+ individuals and/or a positive emphasis on heterosexuality. What might be most shocking to learn is that only 18 states require sex education to be medically accurate. In most schools that teach sex education, the focus is typically on preventing pregnancy, avoiding STIs, and cultivating healthy relationships. These topics are often presented through a cisgender, heterosexual lens and are rarely taught from a sex-positive perspective.

The topics some students are not learning about in their sex education classes are abortion, masturbation, pleasure, and the intersection of race, gender, sexual orientation, and oppression. Schools often see these topics as "controversial," likely because of the large range of values among parents concerning these topics. Even in schools where sex education is being taught, limited time is generally devoted to the subject. Engaging in the conversations outlined in part 2 of this book will help you fill in some of the gaps left by school-based sex education.

The Challenges of Talking to Your Child about Sex

If you're nervous or feeling challenged by the idea of talking with your child about sexuality, don't worry—you're not alone. Let's be honest: these conversations can be difficult or uncomfortable to approach. But the fact is, sexuality is part of our development, and the earlier we begin having developmentally appropriate sexuality conversations, the easier it will be to continue having them in the future.

So why does having these conversations feel so challenging for some parents? Perhaps your parents never talked about sexuality with you, and you don't have a model for what these conversations should look like. That's OK! You're the parent now, and you get to create the model that will work best for you and your child(ren). Maybe you never received formal sex education in school, so you're afraid you won't have the right information or know how to answer your child's questions. This book will provide you with the basic information and prompts you need to start the conversation. Credible websites, such as CDC.gov and HealthyChildren.org, can also help provide additional information when you need it.

If you're counting on your child's school sex education program to teach them all they need to know, you're missing out on the opportunity to bring the lens of your values, beliefs, and racial and cultural identities into the conversations they may be having. If your child identifies as a member of the LGBTQ+ community, you may be struggling with the fact that much of the material available about sexuality is presented from a very heteronormative perspective (assuming that heterosexuality is the "standard" orientation). Throughout this book, I use inclusive language and address issues relevant to the LGBTQ+ community. Maybe your child lives with a physical or cognitive disability. Members of these vulnerable populations are often overlooked or, worse, not seen as sexual beings—but they need the same information any other child does. The primary differences to consider are how you present the information (e.g., daily repetition of skills may be necessary for some individuals) and when (e.g., when is it developmentally appropriate).

If you're a member of the Black, Indigenous, and people of color (BIPOC) communities, you may struggle with addressing the hypersexualization of people of color because it means further exposing your child to the racism that exists in our society. Using teachable moments (addressed later) can be a developmentally appropriate way to start these difficult conversations. Maybe you accept that your child is a sexual being, but you think they're too young to discuss these topics. It's important to anticipate their developmental needs and stay one step ahead. A common analogy used in sex education is that you can't start teaching algebra in middle school without first teaching addition, subtraction, multiplication, and division in elementary school. If you wait until a young person is in their teens to start discussing sexuality, you'll miss many of the developmental building blocks that provide the foundation for these important conversations.

Initiating Conversations

As children grow up, they have many questions about sexual development and relationships, but they don't always feel comfortable asking them. Parents often have to start these important conversations, which can be quite anxiety-provoking for some people. Consider the following practical tips to help set the right tone.

Choose the Right Time and Place

First, make sure both of your schedules will allow sufficient time to have these important conversations. Choose a private, quiet space with minimal distractions so your full attention can be given. Long car rides, subway rides, or long walks are great opportunities to talk—plus, if the topic feels awkward, minimal eye contact is required.

CHALLENGES FOR SINGLE AND FOSTER PARENTS

I'd be remiss if I didn't start this section by expressing the admiration I have for single and foster parents. These are tough jobs, so be kind to yourself! As a single parent, talking about sexuality with your child can feel challenging, especially if your child is of a different gender than you. It's important to provide as much information as possible and share your values and beliefs, but to also recognize that your child may be having certain experiences you just can't relate to. That's OK. Menstruation and spontaneous erections are changes children may feel more comfortable discussing with someone of the same gender. This might be a good time for an aunt, uncle, grandparent, or cousin to help out with the conversation.

Foster parents have the enormous responsibility of caring for a child who may have suffered severe trauma and instability in their lives. Before discussing sexuality, it is important to know if the children in your care are survivors of child sexual abuse or have been removed from the home because of abuse related to their LGBTQ+ identity. In addition to everything the child may be dealing with, puberty and adolescence are still occurring. Foster children need information to understand the changes happening in their body. If the child has grown up in an environment where the values and beliefs are very different from your own, you may face additional challenges when talking about sexuality. In these cases, be sure to explore a range of values, including your own, and encourage the child to talk about their values and how they have formed them. This can help build trust and show that you value their lived experiences.

Use Teachable Moments

Opportunities to discuss important topics related to sexual development and relationships are all around us. They can be found in movies, in music, in magazines, on TV shows, in commercials, online, and in unexpected places. Use scenarios in the media as an opportunity to start a conversation.

Ask Open-Ended Questions

If you ask yes/no questions, you'll likely get yes/no responses, and these may not provide a lot of information. Instead, ask questions like, "What are some qualities you think are important in a romantic relationship? Why?"

Be Open to All Questions

It's important for your child to know that they can talk to you about anything. Ignoring a question or telling them that one is inappropriate sends the message that you're not willing to discuss certain topics. If you need time to think about how you'd like to respond to a tough question, let the child know that, and promise to get back to them.

You Don't Need to Know All the Answers

Some of us may not have had comprehensive sex education, which can make us feel that we don't have all the necessary information to address certain topics. That's OK. If your child asks a question you don't know the answer to, offer to check out a trusted website with your child and find the answer together.

Do More Listening Than Talking

Once your child starts responding to the question(s) you've asked, listen to their responses without interrupting. If they share something that is factually inaccurate or doesn't align with your values, wait until they are finished speaking before you address it. Don't get stuck on the problematic part of the response—focus on hearing *all* of what they are saying.

Stay Calm

If you hear something upsetting during the conversation, take a moment to breathe and collect your thoughts before you respond. Yelling or arguing about a topic will only shut down the conversation, closing the door to understanding why your child feels a certain way and to the opportunity to express your values and expectations.

End on a Positive Note

It's important to end the conversation on a positive note, no matter how it goes. This will leave you both feeling good about the communication you've established and will make it easier for you to have similar conversations in the future. Remember, there is no singular "talk"; conversations about sexual development and relationships are lifelong.

Fielding Questions

Every time I think I've heard every possible question there is, someone will surprise me. One concern I hear from parents is they're afraid they won't know the answer to a question their child asks. Me too—and I've been doing this for 20 years and have talked with thousands of young people. No one could know the answer to every possible question their child may ask, but figuring out what's at the root of their question can be very helpful. Let's start with some basic types of questions and examples of what they might sound like.

- Fact-based questions are the easiest to respond to because clear, factual answers can be found on reputable websites. An example is this: "What is a condom?"
- "Am I normal?" questions may surface if a child is worried about an experience they're having, though they may not want to admit that that is their concern. Some examples include: "Is it normal for one testicle to hang lower than the other?" and "My friend is worried because she didn't

get her period when she was expecting it. She hasn't had sex, so she's not worried about being pregnant. Is that normal?"

- Values-based questions involve seeking advice about perceptions of what is right or wrong. For example, "Is masturbation wrong?" We'll talk more about these types of questions shortly.
- When your child asks permission-seeking questions, they're testing the waters of what you approve or disapprove of. For example, "Is it OK to have sex before marriage?"

Figuring out the underlying motivation behind the question makes it easier for you to respond in a way that provides the answers they really want to know.

Now let's explore how to answer the questions. Although there are no one-size-fits-all responses, you can take some steps to help guide your answer.

- First, acknowledge every question your child asks. Ignoring a question or saying that it's not appropriate is still a response, but remember, we are attempting to remain sex-positive.
- Thank your child for coming to you and trusting you with their question. If you need time to think about how you want to respond, that's OK. Just let them know you'll get back to them with an answer.
- If the question is fact-based, find the answer on a reliable website, like CDC.gov or HealthyChildren.org, and share the answer with them. It's not a good idea to send tweens and teens to find the answer themselves, because they may come across content that is not developmentally appropriate.
- If your child asks a question that has an inaccuracy, you'll want to correct it when you provide the response. For example, "I know *lesbian* means when two boys like each other. What is it called when two girls like each other?"

- For each question, start by answering the factual part of the question, then share your values and beliefs.
- When you respond to your child's questions, be sure to ask meaningful follow-up questions. Think of every question as an opportunity to share your values and beliefs—and, most important, stay calm and positive!

Defining Your Values and Beliefs

The final overarching component to talking with your child(ren) about sexuality is defining your values and beliefs. The best practice in teaching school-based sex education is for the educator to keep their personal values out of the conversation while allowing students time to explore how they feel about a range of topics. For parents, introducing your values and beliefs is essential to these conversations. In chapter 1, I introduced the SOW method, which I adapted for families from a model commonly used in the sex ed field:

Some people believe . . . ,
Other people believe . . . , and
We (your family) believe . . .

After presenting this range of values, ask your child what they think about the topic—then listen.

Before you start defining your values and beliefs with your child, it can be helpful to think about those values and beliefs and how they were developed. Consider your childhood. Was sexuality something that was discussed openly? Did religious or spiritual beliefs inform the values and beliefs of your family? What messages did you receive about sexuality from your peers, TV, and the movies? Even if your parents or caregivers weren't talking about sexuality, their silence or reactions were sending messages, while teachers, peers, and media were sending their own messages as well. All of this is true for your child, too.

The final point to consider is what messages you want to send to your child about sexuality. You hold some values more strongly than others. Share those with your child by framing them using a positive perspective and explaining why they are important to you. If your child has a different perspective, listen and avoid threats—this will only close down future conversations. You probably didn't grow up with all the same values and beliefs as your parents, and your child likely won't grow up with all the same values and beliefs as you, but it's important for them to have a starting point for their own values exploration, except in cases where their beliefs may be harmful to others. In these cases, it is important to be firm with your position.

Content Warning: In the following chapters, you may come across content that conjures up strong mental or emotional responses as a result of past experiences. If this happens, take a break and come back to that content later, or just skip it entirely. However you choose to proceed, please be sure to take care of yourself in whatever way feels most appropriate.

The Conversations

Part 2 provides 70 guided conversations on a wide range of sexuality topics. Sex education has many goals, including helping young people understand how their bodies develop and work; learning how to access sexual health information and resources; developing the skills necessary for healthy and pleasurable platonic and romantic relationships; learning to feel comfortable in their own bodies and with their identities; and learning critical thinking skills. Discussing the full range of sexuality topics can help young people grow up to be empathetic individuals who believe equity and inclusion of all people creates a healthier world where everyone has a right to control their own sexual and reproductive health. These conversations are designed to address these goals.

Growing Up

Chapter 3 provides basic background information and prompts to help you start having sex-positive conversations with the young people in your life. Topics include their changing body, how to meet the needs of their changing body, and identity development.

Normalizing Changes

AGES 8+

The changes of puberty can be very confusing and can cause anxiety for some young people. Some may question whether the changes they are experiencing are normal. They may ask questions like these: "My friend said they are getting boners for no reason all the time. Is there something wrong with him?" or "I know someone whose breasts are growing unevenly. Isn't that weird?" In both cases, these young adolescents may be referring to themselves because they feel shame or embarrassment about their bodies.

It's important to talk honestly and frequently with your child and normalize the changes they're experiencing. Puberty is an experience everyone shares, so keep it light. It's OK to joke about the awkwardness of this stage of life. To the extent possible, try to anticipate the physical changes that may raise concerns for your child and talk about them before they happen. Changes like menstruation and wet dreams can be worrisome to a young person who doesn't know to expect them. Assure your child as much as possible that what they are experiencing is common. If something seems unusual, contact your pediatrician for more information.

After providing information on a specific topic, you may ask:

Questions and Prompts

- What questions do you have about ... ?
- Do you have any concerns about ... ?
- How do you feel about your body going through these changes?
- Do you realize that almost every adult has experienced these changes? How do you think they felt when it happened to them?
- Who are some other adults you trust who you can ask sexuality-related questions if you don't want to ask me?

Remember, no single conversation will meet the needs of your children at every point in their development. Talking about sexuality needs to be a lifelong conversation and should always be done from a positive perspective.

Menstruation

AGES 8–12

Menstruation is the monthly process where the uterus contracts and pushes out the endometrium, the rich lining of blood and tissue that develops in the uterus to support a pregnancy. The typical menstrual cycle is about 24 to 28 days. The cycle is counted from the first day of a person's period up to the first day of their next period. This is an average range and can be longer or shorter for some people, and it's often irregular in frequency when they first start getting their period.

It's common to have a heavier flow of menstrual fluids during the first few days of a person's period. If a person often experiences a heavy flow, it may not be anything to worry about, but consider a visit to your healthcare provider with your child and allow them to discuss what they are experiencing. In the days between ovulation and the start of their period, most people experience symptoms of premenstrual syndrome, or PMS. These may include mood swings, fatigue, food cravings, and tenderness of the breasts. Rest, hot baths, heating pads, exercise, and over-the-counter pain medications can help reduce the pain associated with menstruation.

Questions and Prompts

- What do you know about menstruation/getting your period?
- Do you know why you get a period?
- What are some ways you think you might be able to tell if you're about to get your period?
- Have you had any of these symptoms?
- How do you feel about starting your period?
- What questions do you have about getting your period? Is there anything you're worried about?

Encourage your child to track their period (count the days) and to take notice of any patterns that occur around their menstrual flow. This can help them anticipate their needs regarding period hygiene products.

Pads, Tampons, and Menstrual Cups

AGES 8–12

As menstruation begins, your child will need some type of period hygiene product as a regular part of their personal care. These products include pads, tampons, and menstrual cups. Menstrual pads sit inside the underwear to absorb menstrual fluids as they leave the vagina and should be changed every 3 to 4 hours. Tampons and menstrual cups are inserted into the vagina to absorb or collect menstrual fluid. Tampons need to be changed every 4 to 8 hours, and menstrual cups should be removed and emptied every 8 to 12 hours. Menstrual cups can be purchased in most places period products are sold. Some young people may be less comfortable with tampons and menstrual cups because they involve inserting them into the vagina, so it's important to select a product they are comfortable with.

Pads and tampons should never be reused. Some menstrual cups are for one-time use, while others can be washed and reused. Your child may want to try different options before deciding which they're most comfortable with. It's important for them to know that just because someone they know uses a certain type of period hygiene product, that isn't necessarily the best option for them.

Questions and Prompts

+ What type of menstrual hygiene product do you think you want to try?
+ What are some of the things you think you might like or dislike about each of the options?
+ What do you think are the most important things to remember about using pads, tampons, or menstrual cups?
+ What questions do you have about using . . . ?
+ What is your plan to make sure you always have period products when you need them?

Tampons and pads come in different shapes and sizes and may need to be changed more regularly on days when the person has a heavier flow. Tampons must be changed regularly to avoid serious health issues. Be sure to explain to your child they should always wash their hands before and after changing their period hygiene product.

Spontaneous Erections and Wet Dreams

AGES 10–14

As puberty begins and testosterone enters the body, people AMAB will begin to experience spontaneous erections. They are called "spontaneous erections" because they occur without sexual stimulation (e.g., waking up in the morning, while in a car or on the bus, or just sitting in class). While spontaneous erections can occur several times a day, and they can feel pretty embarrassing for the person experiencing them, they are perfectly normal and will go away on their own.

Additionally, at around age 14, your child may begin to experience nocturnal emissions, commonly referred to as "wet dreams." This is when the penis releases semen through the urethra while the person is sleeping. Wet dreams are also completely normal. If your child doesn't know what a wet dream is, and they experience one, they may assume that they wet the bed and feel ashamed or embarrassed. If your child has a penis, it's important for them to know what spontaneous erections and wet dreams are, that they are normal if they happen and normal if they don't, and that they are nothing to feel embarrassed about.

Questions and Prompts

- Do you know what a spontaneous erection is?
- What questions do you have about spontaneous erections?
- If a spontaneous erection happens at an awkward time, what could you do to make it less noticeable to others?
- Do you know what a wet dream is?
- What questions do you have about wet dreams?

Teens have found many inventive ways of hiding an unwanted erection. These include wearing long shirts to cover their groin area and wearing their pants lower on their hips so they can tuck the erection into their waistband. There's also the time-tested approach of holding something (like a book) in front of you so no one notices.

Masturbation

AGES 10–13

Masturbation can be one of the more challenging topics for parents to discuss with their child. Some people masturbate, others do not. People of all genders may or may not choose to masturbate. Both choices are normal. However it may present some challenges in relation to your personal values.

If you have negative values or feelings about masturbation, explore where those feelings come from. Be honest with your child about why you have these feelings, but keep the conversation positive. Masturbation does not cause any physical harm to an individual. People may masturbate to reduce stress or anxiety or to explore sexual feelings. Masturbation allows an individual to explore what feels good to them in a safe way (they cannot get pregnant or contract an STI from masturbating); this can help them have more pleasurable sexual relationships in the future if they choose. Make sure your child knows that masturbation should always be done in a private place, and they should never masturbate with anything that can cut, harm, or irritate their genitals.

Questions and Prompts

+ Do you know what masturbation is?
+ What are your thoughts/feelings about masturbation?
+ Why do you think some people choose to masturbate, and others do not?
+ Why do you think people have to masturbate in a private space if they choose to do so?
+ What are some things a person should avoid using when they masturbate to make sure they don't hurt themself?

As with other conversations, talking about masturbation could potentially be just as awkward for your child as it is for you. Normalizing conversations about masturbation will help reduce stigma and body shame.

Hygiene and Self-Care

AGES 10–14

The physical changes of puberty will bring about the need for tweens and teens to change their hygiene routines. Showering using warm water, soap, and shampoo to wash away the sweat and bacteria that can cause body odor will become part of their daily routine. If they are very active, showering more than once a day may be necessary.

For tweens and teens who are experiencing acne, special body washes can be used during their shower, and creams may be applied afterward. These products should be used as directed, or they may irritate the skin. Your child also may begin using a deodorant and/or antiperspirant daily (antiperspirants are made to reduce sweating, and deodorants are designed to cover up odor). Shaving facial, body, and/or pubic hair may also become part of their routine. Finally, your child will want to make sure they are changing their clothes daily—including their socks and underwear—to reduce the likelihood of emitting body odor.

Questions and Prompts

- What changes do you think happen during puberty that can affect your hygiene?
- Why do you think it's important to shower at least once daily?
- What do you think would happen if you didn't shower every day?
- How do you feel when you're showered and clean, as opposed to when you're not?
- What do you see as the pros and cons of using an antiperspirant or a deodorant?
- Why do you think it's important to change your clothes, including socks and underwear, every day?

Never shame your child for having body odor. While their hygiene routines are within their control, the odor their body produces is not. Gently encourage them to take a shower if necessary. The goal should be to teach them better hygiene—not to shame them.

Douching

AGES 12+

Working with young people over the years, I've noticed the topic of douching typically comes up in two contexts: (1) Do I need to douche regularly? (2) Does douching after penile-vaginal sex reduce the risk of pregnancy? The answer to both of these questions is no. Douching can actually throw off the balance of the bacteria that live in the vagina and can increase the chances of vaginal infections. Douching after penile-vaginal sex can actually push sperm farther up the vagina and past the cervix, increasing the likelihood of pregnancy. If there is a change in the smell or color of a person's vaginal discharge, they may want to see a healthcare provider.

Questions and Prompts

- What do you know about douching?
- Why do you think a person might want to douche?
- Did you know that most doctors recommend that people with vaginas should not douche?
- Why do you think most doctors don't recommend douching?
- What do you think a person should do if there's a change in the smell or color of their vaginal discharge?
- What do you think could happen if a person douches after penile-vaginal sex?

Commercials for douching products present a great opportunity to start this conversation. Talking about douching as part of menstrual health care, noting that it is not necessary and may be harmful, is another great way to address the topic.

Body Image

AGES 12–16

Body image has to do with how a person sees themself. During puberty, many tweens and teens begin to spend more time noticing the changes that are happening to their body and comparing their body to others' bodies. For people AFAB, the predominant images presented for the "ideal figure" in some cultures include a smaller stature, a small waist, and big breasts. For people AMAB, the predominant images include a larger stature, lots of muscles, and a big penis. We are exposed to these images from the time we are children through the toys we play with (e.g., Barbie dolls, superhero action figures) and the cartoons we watch. It's important to help tweens and teens understand that most of these qualities are determined by genetics, so they have no control over them. You can also explain that many of the images they see in advertisements are edited with programs such as Photoshop.

Questions and Prompts

+ What do you think most people in your school who are your age see as the "ideal" body type?

+ Do you agree that this is what is beautiful?

+ How do you think some people get their bodies to have the "ideal" look?

+ Do you think they get that look in a healthy way?

+ Do you think the pictures of people on social sites are all real?

+ Why do you think pictures in advertisements are altered?

Watch for any changes in your child's diet or exercise routine, along with other changes related to their appearance that become excessive. This may be a sign of the development of an eating disorder or body dysmorphic disorder (a mental illness involving obsessive focus on a perceived flaw in appearance). Talk to your child and your pediatrician if you become concerned about either of these changes.

Self-Esteem

AGES 10+

Self-esteem is more than just feeling good about oneself. It has to do with an individual's sense of self-worth and how valuable they think they are to others. There are many different ideas about how one can help their child build their self-esteem, but consider these core components for helping to build the self-esteem of the young people in your life:

- Establish value for their unique identity and an ability to live by their own standards and values
- Embrace self-acceptance of all their intersecting identities
- Cultivate social acceptance—as humans, we're social beings and need other people
- Acquire a sense of worthiness of all the good things they hope for in life
- Build self-efficacy around the knowledge and skills necessary to be self-sufficient
- Develop a feeling that they have control over their lives, and that they are in control of the direction of their future

Parents can help develop all these components in their child during adolescence by articulating and reinforcing their importance. It's crucial to note that, during puberty, self-esteem can become closely tied to body image because young people are frequently comparing themselves to others.

Questions and Prompts

+ What qualities do you have that you're most proud of?
+ What would your friends say are your best qualities?
+ What do you want the most for your future?
+ Tell me why you deserve those things.
+ [Specify a particular situation, say, an encounter with a teacher] didn't work out this time, but let's think about what you can do to make things work out better next time.
+ Do you feel like you're in control of this situation?
+ How can you accept the things that are not in your control?

Love, support, and acceptance from parents are foundational to helping a child develop many of the components that contribute to high self-esteem. Giving your child greater autonomy and responsibility as they get older also provides them with the opportunity to develop a clearer sense of who they are as an individual and to develop self-efficacy in basic life skills.

Emotional Intelligence

AGES 8+

Emotional intelligence involves identifying, exploring, and managing our feelings as they relate to ourselves and others. The five key components of emotional intelligence are self-awareness, self-regulation, social skills, empathy, and motivation. Unlike our IQs, which level off at a certain point in our lives, research tells us that our emotional intelligence continues to develop throughout our lives. Research also suggests that high emotional intelligence can be a greater contributing factor to a person's success than their IQ.

Working to develop emotional intelligence early can help improve a young person's decision-making and relationship skills. You can help develop your child's emotional intelligence in many ways, such as teaching them to identify emotions and put a name to them, validating that it is OK to feel a wide range of emotions, encouraging them to think about what makes them feel better when they experience negative emotions, and exploring how their emotions impact other people.

Questions and Prompts

- (When their volume and rate of speech increase, ask) What are you feeling right now that is causing this to happen?
- How are you feeling right now?
- What caused you to feel this way?
- What techniques have you used in the past to calm yourself or make yourself feel better?
- How do you think the way you expressed your emotions impacted [insert names]?
- (When watching TV or a movie) How do you think [this character] is feeling? How do you feel about their situation?

Young people may not always want to talk about their emotions in the moment. That's OK. Give them time to process the current circumstances, then come back and reflect on what happened. Remember, every emotion is valid and should never be ignored.

Changing Social Groups

AGES 11+

As children enter middle school and explore their identity, it's common for them to grow apart from their earlier childhood friends and move in and out of different social circles. These changes may be due to their changing interests or the changing interests of their friends, and it can be particularly difficult when their friends' interests change and they feel left behind.

Normalizing and accepting these changes is important for your child's social adjustment and self-esteem. Tajfel and Turner's social identity theory (1979) presents three stages of social change: categorization (putting people into groups that tell us something about them, such as race, sexual identity, etc.); social identification (adopting the identity of the group[s] we assign ourselves to); and social comparison (seeing if the identity of the group[s] we are in compares well to other groups). Moving through these stages is a common process that happens repeatedly throughout our lifetime.

Questions and Prompts

- I noticed you're not hanging out with [name(s)] anymore. What happened?
- How do you feel about not hanging out with [name(s)] anymore?
- Who is [name of the child's new friend(s)]? How did you meet them?
- What do you like about [name(s)]? What do you have in common with them?
- What do you and [name(s)] like to do when you hang out?
- How does [name(s)] treat you when you're hanging out?
- Do you feel any pressure to do things you don't want to do when you hang out with [name(s)]?

As children get older, they may become more private regarding what they want to share about their friend groups. It's important to balance their privacy with their safety by building a trusting relationship, and setting and enforcing clear boundaries and expectations. Your child needs to know they can always come to you about anything.

Intersecting Identities

AGES 15+

Many identities develop during adolescence that define who we are as individuals and how we move through the world; our sexual identity is just one of them. Kimberlé Crenshaw created the theory of intersectionality in 1989 to describe how race, class, gender, and other individual characteristics "intersect" with one another and overlap. Similar research explains how the bodies of young Fem, Black, Latina, and Asian-Pacific Islander girls have long been hypersexualized in comparison to those of their white peers, leading to false negative stereotypes and potentially tragic outcomes (e.g., Black women are statistically less likely to be believed when they report sexual violence).

A person's gender, ethnicity, religion, and other identities also have an impact on how they move through the world and how others react to them. Oftentimes, our society exhibits a double standard concerning the sexual behavior of people AMAB, which is often encouraged and celebrated, compared to the sexual behavior of people AFAB, which is often discouraged and shamed. All these different lenses impact our sexual identity. It's important to discuss how dangerous hypersexualizing others is to help create an environment where all people are free to develop positive sexual identities.

Questions and Prompts

- What sexual stereotypes have you heard about people of our race, ethnicity, religion, etc.? What about people in other groups?
- Where do you think those stereotypes come from?
- Do you think stereotypes can be dangerous? Why or why not?
- How do you feel when you hear those stereotypes?
- How do you respond when other people verbalize those stereotypes?
- How do you think other people feel when they hear those things being said about them?
- What do you think you should do if you hear other people saying negative things about people of a different race, ethnicity, religion, etc.?

Consider discussing how ableism, anti-Semitism, homophobia, racism, transphobia, xenophobia, and any form of hatred against another human is dangerous. During your conversation, see if you can brainstorm examples of how perpetuating negative stereotypes, including sexual stereotypes about whole communities, can risk them harm.

Coming Out

AGES 8+

Each individual should be fully in control of making decisions about when, where, and how to come out of the closet about their sexual orientation or gender identity. It's important not to pressure your child into putting a label on their sexual orientation or gender identity or into coming out before they're ready. When your child does come out, thank them for sharing this very personal piece of their identity with you and be direct about your love and support for them. Be aware that your child coming out to you does not necessarily mean they're fully ready to discuss all aspects of their sexual or gender identity at that time. The most important thing you can do is let your child know they are loved and be there for support until they're ready to share this piece of their lives with you. Also, never share your child's sexual identity with someone else without their permission.

Questions and Prompts

* Is it OK if I ask questions to learn more about how you're feeling?
* How are you feeling now that you've shared this with me?
* How long have you known this about yourself?
* Have you come out to anyone else yet? If so, how did they respond?
* (Related to sexual orientation) Do you have romantic feelings for anyone special?
* (Related to gender identity) Have you given any thought to whether or how you'd like to affirm your gender? (For instance, is there another name you would like me to address you by?)
* How can I support you in your coming-out journey?

Keep in mind that there's no single path to the development of one's sexual or gender identity, so this may be a fluid and nonlinear path for an individual. Follow your child's lead in the process, and respect when, how, and whether they want to discuss it.

Exploring Sexual Identity

AGES 9+

Much of our world can be considered heteronormative—meaning heterosexuality is promoted as the norm—but there are many different sexual identities. Some of the most common are lesbian, gay, bisexual, asexual, pansexual, demisexual (attraction based on emotional bonds), and queer. It's most important to ask your child what their identity means to them and be supportive of that.

Although many models of identity development exist, it may be helpful to consider that it happens in stages. Generally, people may move from stages of confusion around their identity to comparison with others to tolerance of their identity, and then they eventually experience acceptance, pride, and integration of their identity with their full self.

Questions and Prompts

◆ Is it OK for me to ask questions to learn more about your identity?

◆ What does being [identity] mean to you?

◆ How does labeling this part of your identity feel?

◆ What excites you the most about having this identity?

◆ Do you have any concerns about having this identity?

◆ How do you want me to talk about your sexual identity with you moving forward?

◆ Would you like me to look into opportunities for you to meet other young people who share your identity?

Never reveal your child's sexual identity to others without their permission. To reach the LGBT National Hotline, call 888-843-4564. If a young person is in crisis, feeling suicidal, or in need of a safe and judgment-free place to talk, call the Trevor Lifeline at 866-488-7386.

Exploring Gender Identity

AGES 8+

We live in what many consider to be a cisnormative world, meaning the assumption is that most people's gender identity matches their sex assigned at birth. While conversations may begin earlier, it becomes particularly important to discuss gender identity with a questioning child before the physical changes of puberty begin.

In 2004, Arlene Istar Lev developed the transgender emergence model that lays out typical stages of gender identity development. The stages in this model are awareness, seeking information/reaching out, disclosure to significant others, exploration regarding identity and self-labeling, exploration regarding transition issues and possible body modification, and integration (acceptance and post-transition issues). Some people may wish to pursue body modification, including gender-affirming surgery; some may wish to live as their true gender through their clothing and other forms of gender expression; and others may simply wish to acknowledge who they are and have their identity respected by others. It's important not to make assumptions about what your child wants for themself.

Questions and Prompts

- Is it OK for me to ask questions to learn more about your identity?
- What pronouns would you like me to use when referring to you?
- Is there another name you'd like me to use when referring to you?
- How do you feel now that you've shared this information with me?
- How are you feeling about your body changing during puberty?
- Would you like me to explore medical options that can slow down these changes?
- Are there other changes you'd like to make, such as in your clothing or hairstyle, that I can support you with?
- Would you like me to discuss your transition with your school? If so, what information are you OK with me sharing?

It is respectful to always use the name and pronouns your child identifies with. Let your child know that you might not always get all terms and concepts correct at first, but you're open to learning, and any mistakes you might make are a result of your own lack of education regarding the topic.

Puberty Blockers

AGES 8–10

Puberty blockers are medications that temporarily stop the production of estrogen and testosterone, the hormones responsible for many of the physical changes that occur during puberty. These medications are most commonly prescribed by an endocrinologist and are approved by the US Food and Drug Administration (FDA). Puberty blockers are not permanent, so if a person discontinues the medication, their body will begin developing sex hormones again. Although hormone development can resume after discontinuing puberty-blocking medications, it's important to see an endocrinologist early in puberty because they cannot undo physical changes that have already started (e.g., breast development). There are two kinds of puberty blockers:

- A flexible rod called histrelin acetate, which goes under the skin of the arm and lasts for one year
- A shot called leuprolide acetate, which works for one, three, or four months at a time

Questions and Prompts

- What do you know about puberty blockers?
- What questions do you have about puberty blockers?
- Is this something you would like to learn more about from a doctor?
- What do you see as the pros and cons of using puberty blockers?
- What do you think are some of the factors we should consider as we make this decision with our healthcare provider?
- How are you feeling about exploring this option?
- What concerns do you have?

Puberty blockers are an option intended to allow more time for a young person to explore their identity without the pressure of the onset of pubertal physical changes. Not all insurance plans will cover puberty-blocking treatment, so be sure to do your research before you begin the process.

Gender Expression

AGES 11+

As children enter middle school, new desires and pressures to express their identity and individuality emerge. One way they may do this is through expressing their gender. Gender expression refers to the external ways all people present their gender to others—for example, through the clothes we wear, the hairstyles we choose, the use or nonuse of makeup and jewelry, and so on. Our society generally sees gender expression as a binary of the feminine and the masculine; however, there are many genders and many ways to express gender. It's perfectly normal for young people to experiment with different ways of expressing their gender as they grow up (e.g. nail polish, makeup, or earrings), and at a glance, we never know everything about a person's sexual orientation or gender identity based on their gender expression.

Questions and Prompts

- I like your [clothing/makeup/etc.]. How did you decide on your look for today?

- How does it make you feel to wear your [clothing/makeup/etc.]? Do you feel this way as a result of wearing the clothes, or did the feeling lead you to choose those clothes? (End with a supportive statement.)

- What message are you hoping your [clothing/makeup/etc.] will send to others about who you are?

- Did a celebrity provide any inspiration for your outfit? If so, who? What do you admire about them?

- How do the other kids at school like your look? Does anyone else have a similar look?

- What other clothing/makeup items do you wish you had to better express who you are?

Gender expression that does not align with society's gender role expectations—how society generally believes a man or a woman should look or behave—is a common cause of bullying. All children should learn that everyone deserves to be treated with kindness and respect no matter how they dress.

Intersex Variations

AGES 11+

Intersex is an umbrella term used to refer to a variety of conditions in which a person's reproductive and/or sexual anatomy differs from the typically expected anatomy. You may have previously heard such a person referred to as a "hermaphrodite," but that is a medically inaccurate and offensive term. Sometimes the variations may be visible at birth, but oftentimes they are not, since intersex variations can be related to internal organs, hormones, and/or chromosomes. Puberty is a time when intersex variations that involve internal organs may become evident. For example, a person born with an underdeveloped uterus, or without a uterus, may not get a period. Additionally, if the variation is at the chromosome level, a person can go for much or all of their life without knowing they are intersex. Statistically, 1 in every 2,000 people are born with intersex variations.

Questions and Prompts

- Do you know what *intersex* means?
- Did you know that there are many different natural variations that could make a person intersex?
- Did you know that being intersex is much more common than most people think?
- Are intersex variations talked about as part of your sex education class at school?
- Why do you think it's important to talk about the fact that some people are intersex?

Intersex variations are natural variations, and most do not require any kind of medical treatment. Parents and doctors are strongly discouraged from doing any kind of surgery on an intersex newborn unless it is medically necessary (in most cases, it is not). To learn more about intersex variations, visit the website for the Intersex Society of North America at ISNA.org.

Nurturing Relationships to Thrive

Chapter 4 provides information and prompts to help you start having sex-positive conversations with the young people in your life about the many complicated dynamics and emotions that can come into play in their relationships. While a number of the topics are specific to romantic relationships, many can be applied to any relationship (e.g., families, friendships, and professional relationships).

First Love

AGES 12+

Did you have a first love, and do you remember them? If so, the person probably had a significant emotional impact on you. You may even still be with them! Experiencing love for the first time is a key milestone in most people's lives, yet I often hear adults refer to young people's relationships as "puppy love" or other terms that minimize their significance.

In many ways, a young person's first loving romantic relationship can set the tone for how their future relationships will evolve. Issues concerning trust and vulnerability are important at every age. As the primary sex educator in your child's life, you never want to diminish the magnitude of the emotions they are experiencing in any romantic relationship. If their first love relationship comes to an end, it may be truly crushing, so don't just tell them to brush it off—help them process the emotions they're feeling. If they don't want to talk right away, give them time, and make yourself available when they're ready.

Questions and Prompts

+ How do you feel when you're with [name]?
+ Do you feel happy and safe when you're with [name]?
+ Do you trust [name]?
+ When can we talk about how you're feeling?
+ It's OK to feel [emotion]. Let's talk about it.

Start asking questions about your child's romantic partners early on in the relationship, just not in an interrogating way. It shows you're interested in learning about them and you're supportive of the relationship. It also normalizes having conversations about romantic relationships and sends the message they don't have to be kept secret.

Resolving Conflicts

AGES 10+

The ability to resolve conflicts is another important skill young people need to learn in order to thrive in their relationships. Since conflicts can sometimes intensify our emotions, it's often best for everyone involved to take some time and space to decompress and reflect on the situation before trying to reach a resolution. This isn't always possible, but it's a great starting point when it can be done. Sometimes conflicts can be resolved through a simple fact-finding mission (e.g., "Tell you what—let's look it up on the Internet."). Other times, conflict involves a difference of values or beliefs and can be harder to resolve. In these situations, it's important for everyone to actively listen to each other and try to negotiate a solution that is best for the relationship (that is, if the relationship is worth maintaining). The most important lesson young people need to learn about conflict is that it is never OK to bring any type of violence into a dispute.

Questions and Prompts

+ Do you know what *conflict resolution* means?
+ What are some ways people might try to resolve a conflict?
+ Why do you think a person should never use violence to resolve a conflict?
+ How are conflicts resolved within your group of friends?
+ What do you think people should do if they get really (angry, sad, etc.) during a conflict?
+ What are some things that aren't worth fighting over?

When there is conflict in your home, model positive examples of how to resolve it. Pull out the dictionary and see if the word someone used in Scrabble really is a word! If emotions are high and the conflict cannot be resolved by facts, insist that everyone take some time to cool down and get into a space where they can calmly discuss the situation.

Emotional Intimacy

AGES 13+

Emotional intimacy involves the feelings of closeness and safety between people that allows them to feel more connected to each other. Emotional intimacy requires a certain level of vulnerability and trust, so it is not developed quickly. Emotional intimacy can't be forced, and once it is achieved, it should always be treated with care. For some people, allowing themselves to be vulnerable or to trust others can be very difficult. Emotional intimacy doesn't just exist within romantic relationships; it can also exist within families and friendships. Young people who grow up in a home where emotional intimacy is absent because of abuse, neglect, or any other type of trauma may struggle to develop it in their romantic relationships. This may also be true for young people who are in the foster care system and frequently moved from family to family.

Questions and Prompts

- Do you know what *emotional intimacy* means?
- How do you think people develop emotional intimacy?
- How do you know if you have emotional intimacy with someone?
- What do you think emotional intimacy looks like in a relationship?
- Do you think a person can develop emotional intimacy if they don't feel safe in their relationship or have only talked with the person online?
- Can you think of some reasons a person might not allow themselves to be vulnerable with someone else?

Serial dating, fear of commitment, and difficulty with physical contact or expressing needs are all signs that a person may be struggling with emotional intimacy issues. To support someone who is exhibiting these signs, encourage them to practice self-compassion, pay attention to their thoughts and feelings, and try to identify where they are coming from. Also recommend that they consider seeing a mental health professional who can work with them on the issue.

Communication in Relationships

AGES 12+

Effective communication is not always easily accomplished in relationships. Young people benefit from knowing the difference between active and passive listening, with the goals of being an active listener and knowing how to tell if someone is actively listening to them. They also need to know about the three types of communication: passive, aggressive, and assertive. Passive communication is characterized by avoiding confrontation and not expressing thoughts and feelings; aggressive communication is often harsh and does not necessarily involve respecting the rights of others; and assertive communication is typically direct and respectful. Each of these has a place in conversation, so the skill is to not only learn how to use each of these types of communication, but to also know when it might be appropriate to use each one. As if that's not complicated enough, throw texting and other forms of written communication into the mix, and take the tone of voice and facial expressions out of the picture, and things can get even more tricky. Clear communication is essential.

Questions and Prompts

- Do you know what active listening is?
- How can you tell if someone is actively listening to what you're saying?
- How can you show someone that you're actively listening to them?
- Do you know what passive communication, aggressive communication, and assertive communication are?
- When might you use passive, aggressive, or assertive communication?
- How can people's facial expressions help you know what they might be feeling during a conversation?
- How can you tell how someone might be feeling when you're communicating through text messages?

Model active listening with your child by nodding, summarizing what you are hearing them say, and asking follow-up questions. Use a previous text message conversation between you and your child to explore how tone of voice and facial expressions can be translated into text to try to minimize confusion. It's a great opportunity to also learn what all those emojis mean.

Showing Affection

AGES 12+

As young people start to explore romantic relationships, it's important for them to know there are many ways they can show a romantic partner they care. For younger adolescents, holding hands, hugging, or putting their arm around a person may be physical ways of showing affection. Writing a letter expressing how they feel about their partner, taking selfies together, or just spending time together doing things they enjoy are nonphysical ways of showing affection. As they get older, a message young people deserve to continue receiving is that there are many ways of showing affection to a romantic partner that do not involve having sex. They also need to know that if someone asks them to do something to "prove" their love, and they are not comfortable with it, they should not feel pressured to do it.

Questions and Prompts

- Do you know what it means to show affection to someone?
- Do you think you need to ask consent if you're going to show affection to someone?
- How do you think showing affection with a friend or family member might be different than showing affection for a romantic partner?
- What are some nonphysical ways people can show affection to each other?
- Do you think everyone shows affection in the same way?
- Do you think a person should ever be forced to prove their affection?

Model both physical and nonphysical ways of showing your child affection. If you tend to hug a lot already, maybe leave them a little note to express your feelings or give them a card for no reason other than to express your thoughts and feelings.

Jealousy

AGES 13+

Jealousy is an interesting emotion to discuss with teens. Some teens think jealousy is a positive sign in a relationship because it shows their partner cares. Other teens are completely turned off by the display of jealousy in their relationship because they feel it's a way for their partner to control them. Jealousy can be managed in small amounts, but it can also be extremely dangerous when it gets out of control. It's important to talk about jealousy with young people and help them see when this emotion might raise red flags in a relationship.

Questions and Prompts

- What do you think it means when a partner gets jealous in a relationship?
- Would you like it if someone you were dating was jealous in your relationship?
- Do you see any positive aspects to a partner being jealous?
- Do you think a person can get too jealous in a relationship?
- What are some signs that a person's jealousy might be getting out of hand?
- Have you ever felt jealous in a relationship? If so, how did you handle it?

The amount of jealousy that is acceptable in a relationship depends on each individual. Regardless of how little or how much jealousy a person is willing to tolerate, they need to know that there's a point where too much jealousy can become unhealthy and even dangerous. Be sure to pair your conversations about jealousy with a conversation about power and control in relationships.

Equitable Relationships

AGES 13+

Equity within a relationship means there is shared power and respect among the people involved. An equitable relationship involves mutual support emotionally, financially, and in all aspects of the relationship. It means that when one partner is down, the other is there for them and vice versa. In an equitable relationship, those involved resolve conflict peacefully and with respect for the other person. An equitable relationship also means that those involved feel physically and emotionally safe with each other. Children who grow up in homes where there is abuse often repeat the cycle in their own relationships because they believe violence is a normal part of a relationship. Being in an equitable relationship reduces the likelihood of abuse in that relationship, so it's important to talk about—and model—equitable relationships for young people.

Questions and Prompts

◆ Do you know what equitable means?

◆ What are some of the characteristics of an equitable relationship?

◆ Why is it important for there to be equity between partners in a relationship?

◆ What do you think might happen if there isn't equity in a relationship?

◆ What are some qualities of a relationship where there isn't equity between the people involved?

◆ Do you think having equity in relationships applies only to romantic relationships? Why or why not?

Equity is important in all relationships, including relationships between same-gender couples. To reach the National Domestic Violence Hotline, call 800-799-SAFE (7233) or text START to 88788.

Power Dynamics in Relationships

AGES 13+

In an equitable relationship, a balance of power exists between those involved. However, when there is an imbalance of power and the person with more power takes advantage of it, the relationship can quickly become abusive. An imbalance of power dynamics in a relationship can be rooted in age, gender, race, financial status, immigration status, physical and/or cognitive ability, sexual orientation, gender identity, and many other factors. In an abusive situation, any of these factors can be used to coerce or control the partner who has less power in the relationship. For example, if a person is dating someone older, and the younger person's parents don't know about the relationship, an abusive partner might threaten to reveal the relationship if their partner doesn't do what they want. A person in this type of relationship might feel as if there's no way out, which is why it's so important for your child to know that they can talk to you about anything.

Questions and Prompts

- What do you think it means to have power in a relationship?
- Do you think people always share the same amount of power in a relationship? Why or why not?
- What are some factors that might give a person more power in a relationship?
- Have you ever noticed that, in some relationships, people don't have equal power?
- How do you think an imbalance of power would affect a relationship?
- What advice would you give to a person in a relationship where someone was being abusive with their power?

When discussing power and control, it's important to also talk about how technology is sometimes used as an instrument to control others. Examples are texting a partner to find out where they are or who they are with; leveraging the ability to provide transportation as a way of controlling a partner; and constantly asking about the people who are following and commenting on the person's social media posts.

Hooking Up

AGES 13+

People ascribe many different meanings to *hooking up*, depending on their age and even the community where they live. For some, it means kissing and making out; for others, it means engaging in oral, anal, or vaginal sex. Chances are, young people who go to the same school share a common understanding of what the term means. The ambiguity of this phrase can become problematic, however, when two people have an agreement that they're going to "hook up," and they each have a different understanding of the term's meaning. Even if they both understand it as just kissing or making out, young people should only hook up with someone if they feel ready to do so. Young people also need to know that, similar to the misconception that everyone is having sex, not everyone is hooking up.

Questions and Prompts

- What does *hooking up* mean?
- Does hooking up mean the same thing to everyone?
- How would two people know whether they had the same understanding of what it means to hook up? Do you think you need to get consent before hooking up?
- Do you think everyone is hooking up, or do they just say that they are?
- What would a person say or do if they didn't want to hook up with someone else?

If you hear a term the kids are using but don't know what it means, check out UrbanDictionary.com. You'll probably find the answer (and it will probably be dripping in sarcasm). I have to do my due diligence here and warn you: This site is not for the faint of heart. There is a lot of NSFW (not suitable for work) content, so you'll want to check it out on your cell or home computer in a private area.

Ending a Relationship

AGES 13+

Ending a relationship may be complicated. If someone has ended a relationship with your child, they may feel hurt or rejected. If your child is the one ending the relationship, they might feel relieved and/or sad. During my years working in schools, I heard about a lot of pretty harsh breakup methods. Some students would have their new partner tell their former partner that the relationship is over; others would send a text; and some would just change their social media profile status to SINGLE and never say a word to their "ex."

Young people need to know a few things about ending a relationship. First, if they are in any kind of physical danger, they should talk to an adult to figure out the safest way to end the relationship. Second, it's fine to move on if they're done with a relationship, but they should at least tell their partner it's over, face-to-face if possible. Finally, if someone ends the relationship with them, as tough as it may be, they need to respect that person's decision. Encourage your child to give themself the time and space they need to feel better.

Questions and Prompts

- If a person wants to end a relationship with another person, what are some respectful ways to do that?
- If someone wanted to break up with you, how would you want them to do it?
- What are some signs that it might be time to end a relationship?
- What should a person do if they want to get out of an abusive relationship?
- Do you think a person should try to change their partner's mind if the partner breaks up with them? Why or why not?
- What advice would you give to someone whose partner just broke up with them?

Have your teen practice how they might break up with someone, even if they're not in a relationship. This is especially important for young people who may not be very assertive in their communication style. Practicing what they might say in advance gives them the tools they need to verbalize their decisions more confidently in the future.

Rejection

AGES 12+

Unfortunately, experiencing rejection is part of growing up—it may be rejection from an extracurricular activity, sports team, college or university, or a romantic crush or partner. Accepting rejection is an important skill for all young people to learn. The "It wasn't meant to be" speech may sound good at the time, but turning rejection into a teachable moment will help them develop resilience as they grow. Remind your child they must respect the wishes of the individual or group who has turned them down, and, at some point, they will be the person turning someone else down.

Questions and Prompts

+ Have you ever been rejected by someone or by an organization? If so, how did that make you feel?
+ How do you think other people feel when they are rejected?
+ What do you think would make getting rejected a little easier?
+ Have you ever had to reject someone? If so, how did they respond?
+ How do you think it feels/how did it feel to be the person who has to do the rejecting?
+ What do you think is the best way to respond if someone rejects you?

Rejection can bring on feelings similar to grief. Working through the stages of grief (as presented in the Kübler-Ross model) include working through denial, anger, bargaining, depression, and, eventually, acceptance. Helping your child identify and process these emotions can build emotional intelligence and become a process they use for coping with rejection in the future.

Negotiation

AGES 10+

Negotiation skills are important for young people to develop. For most relationships to thrive, everyone involved must be able to compromise at one point or another. Chances are, negotiations are happening all the time in your home (e.g., what movie to watch together or what toppings to get on the pizza). A young person needs to learn effective communication skills and decision-making skills, and acquire the ability to build trust and rapport with others and to weigh the pros and cons of a given situation. In most negotiations, finding a win-win outcome in which everyone involved gets something they want from the situation should be a goal—for example, "We get half the pizza with your choice of topping, and half with mine." However, your child also needs to know that in some negotiations, outcomes might be win-lose ("I get the topping I want on the whole pizza") or lose-lose ("We don't get pizza at all"), and they should also be encouraged to walk away when something is not up for negotiation at all.

Questions and Prompts

- Do you know what *negotiation* means?
- How do you think people negotiate?
- Why do you think it's important to be able to negotiate?
- Do you know what win-win, win-lose, and lose-lose outcomes are?
- What are some things a person should never negotiate over?

The next time something is up for negotiation at home, be intentional about modeling your negotiation skills, and talk out your thought process so your child can hear the strategy behind it. Try to aim for different outcomes (win-win/win-lose/lose-lose) whenever possible, and model how a person might walk away from a negotiation.

Recognizing Abuse

AGES 13+

Feeling physically and emotionally safe is essential in all relationships: family relationships, friendships, romantic relationships, and others. Young people need to know it's *never*

OK to feel unsafe with a romantic partner. The ability to recognize the signs of physical, emotional, psychological, sexual, and financial abuse can be a lifesaving skill, so it's important to help young people learn this. Young people also need to be able to recognize the cycle of abuse. This cycle typically consists of a period in which tension builds, eventually leading to a major event, such as a verbal or physical altercation. The abusive partner then shows remorse, apologizes, and may promise it will never happen again. Eventually, the tension begins to build again, and the cycle repeats.

Questions and Prompts

- Do you know what physical, emotional, psychological, sexual, and financial abuse are?
- What do you think are some of the signs of [type of abuse]?
- Did you know that there's often a pattern to abuse in relationships?
- Why do you think some people stay in abusive relationships?
- What advice would you give to a friend who was in an abusive relationship?

Abuse can happen via electronic communication just as easily as it can in person. Partners texting WHERE ARE YOU? or WHO ARE YOU WITH? constantly; calling until you pick up; asking you to text them a picture of what you're wearing; saying hurtful and demeaning things through text; and many other actions constitute abusive behaviors. Young people need to know that anything considered abusive in person is also considered abusive online or electronically.

Reporting Sexual Assault

AGES 8+

Every 68 seconds, another American is sexually assaulted. Young people between the ages of 12 and 34 have the highest risk of sexual assault. Transgender, queer, gender-nonconforming ind-viduals, and Indigenous peoples also experience sexual assault at high rates. Too often, sexual assault goes unreported. Only 310 out of every 1,000 sexual assaults are reported to police. Survivors of sexual violence may choose not to report the crime for many reasons. It's important for every person to know that they have options if they, or someone they know, are sexually assaulted. These include filing a report with the police, going to the hospital or a medical center, or calling a victims' advocate to discuss their options. Always believe a person who tells you they've been sexually assaulted, and remind them that it was not their fault, no matter what happened. To contact the National Sexual Assault Hotline, call 800-656-4673.

Questions and Prompts

- Do you know that two-thirds of all sexual assaults go unreported?
- Why do you think a person would choose not to report sexual assault?
- Do you know what the different immediate response options are for people who have been sexually assaulted?
- What options would you tell a friend about if they were sexually assaulted?
- Why do you think it's important for more people to report sexual assault?

The Circle of Six, or Circulo, is an app that allows a person to add up to six people from their contacts to join their circle. If the individual needs help, they can send their GPS coordinates to the circle for a ride, to ask someone from the circle to call them, or to obtain direct access to other resources.

Sex: The Behaviors and the Societal Constructs

We can't talk about sexuality without talking about sex. Chapter 5 provides a wide range of information and prompts on everything from the options available if a pregnancy occurs to the societal constructs that produce shame and stigma. Though some of these conversations could tie together nicely, remember that you'll need to have many of them, so don't try to get everything in at once.

Abstinence

AGES 11+

Abstinence means "voluntarily choosing to refrain from engaging in a behavior—in this case, sexual behavior—for a given period." This means a person can be abstinent for a period of time, then be involved in a sexual relationship, and then return to being abstinent. Abstinence is the only 100-percent effective way to avoid pregnancy and STIs. For sexual health purposes, it's important for young people to understand that abstinence is not just about penile-vaginal sex. A young person may not be engaging in penile-vaginal sex, but if they are participating in oral sex, they can acquire an STI and/or transmit it to a partner.

Questions and Prompts

◆ Do you know what *abstinence* means with regard to sexual behavior?

◆ What do you think are some of the benefits of being abstinent?

◆ Do you think it's realistic for teens to be sexually abstinent? Why or why not?

◆ When do you think a person might choose not to be abstinent anymore?

◆ What do you think about abstinence as a choice for you?

It's important to share your values and expectations with your child when it comes to abstinence. You may hold the value and expectation they will wait to have sex until they are in a long-term, committed relationship, but consider this: According to the US Census Bureau, as of 2020, the average age of first marriage in the United States is around 30 (this includes the average for same-gender couples). Also, not everyone chooses to get married.

Affirming Sexual Curiosity

AGES 13+

As puberty begins, most young people will become curious about sex. Adults often acknowledge the pressures and the influence of media, but they miss one of the key factors: the sudden introduction of sexual hormones into the body. It's typical for young people to begin to express sexual curiosity, and, keeping in mind that some people are asexual, it is also typical if they do not. This is the time to let your sex positivity shine! Put those skills in answering questions into practice. Remember, ignoring or discouraging questions or saying they're inappropriate sends a message that you're not open to talking about certain topics. Let your child know that you're willing to discuss sexuality-related topics, and let them know that it's perfectly fine to be curious about sexuality. If you don't answer their questions, someone else will, and that person's answers may not be accurate or reflect your values.

Questions and Prompts

* I'm guessing that you might have some questions about sex. What are your friends or other people at school saying about it?

* Do you think your friends talk to their parents about sex? Why or why not?

* Why do you think people start to become curious about sex at your age?

* It's important for us to be able to talk about sex openly. What would make talking about this in the future more comfortable for you?

* What questions do you think your friends have about sex?

If your child isn't open to talking about sex, make the conversation about someone else—even if it's a fictional someone else. You can say things like, "I had a friend growing up who always . . ." or "What do you think your friends would say about that?" You'll also have those teachable moments to help start the conversations.

Handling Peer Pressure

AGE 10+

Young people experience peer pressure in a lot of different areas, such as tobacco, alcohol, other drugs, and, likely, sex. Teaching young people different strategies for saying no when they're being pressured is one part of the equation. For example, they may suggest doing something other than what they're being pressured to do, leave the situation completely, or just simply say no. All these strategies can be helpful, but another essential element is teaching young people to hear and accept when someone says no and not to continue pressuring them.

Questions and Prompts

+ Have you ever seen someone being pressured to do something they didn't want to do? If so, how did they respond?

+ How did the person who was pressuring them respond when they said they didn't want to [insert behavior]?

+ How do you think it makes a person feel when they're being pressured to do something they don't want to do?

+ How do you think you would feel if someone was pressuring you?

+ What are some strategies you think a person could use to get out of a situation if they were being pressured to do something they didn't want to do?

+ How can you make sure you're not pressuring other people to do things they do not want to do?

The Construct of Virginity

AGES 13+

Virginity is a societal construct that often puts a lot of pressure on people AFAB to refrain from having penile-vaginal sex; it is more flexible for people AMAB. Young people often have questions about this concept. *What does* virginity *mean? Is it only about someone having penile-vaginal sex?* That is the heteronormative version of the definition. *What about people who never have penile-vaginal sex? Are they virgins forever? What about people who only have oral sex? Are they virgins?* They can still acquire and transmit STIs. *Does losing one's virginity mean the breaking of the hymen?* The hymen can be broken using a tampon, or even riding a bike. *If a person with a penis never penetrates a vagina, are they a virgin forever? If a person is forced to have sex without their consent, are they still a virgin? How about a person with disabilities who can't have penile-vaginal sex; does that mean they will always be a virgin?* These are all questions young people may grapple with, but the bigger questions to consider are *Why does it matter?* and *Who does it matter to?*

Questions and Prompts

- Do people at your school ever talk about virginity? If so, what do they say?
- Do you think different people have different definitions of what it means to be a virgin?
- Do you think young people feel pressure to stay virgins? Where does that pressure come from?
- Do you think people can tell if another person is a virgin? How?
- Why do you think people care if someone else is a virgin?
- Why do you think it's important to talk to a sexual partner about what they think virginity means?

It is beneficial for young people to know that the definition of what makes a person a virgin varies from individual to individual. When talking with a partner about possibly engaging in sexual behaviors, each partner needs to define beforehand what they mean by virginity; this is important because a potential partner may have engaged in behaviors that would allow them to acquire, and then transmit, an STI, but still consider themself a virgin.

Knowing When You're Ready

AGES 12+

With all the pressure and sexual messages surrounding sex, one of the most common questions I have received from young people during my career is this: "How will I know when I'm ready to have sex?" As an educator, I always respond by stating that this is a very personal decision, and instructing them to talk with a trusted adult to learn about that adult's values/beliefs and the values/beliefs of their community (cultural, spiritual, etc.) regarding sex. That's where you come in! This is where you should discuss your values and beliefs (remember the SOW method) and discuss some of the key factors in making this decision. Possible questions you can ask your child: *Do you want to have sex? Why do you want to have sex? Do you have open and honest conversations with your partner about sex? Have you discussed your sexual histories? How will you reduce your risk of pregnancy and/or STIs? Have you discussed your expectations, desires, and limits? Do you trust them? Do you feel physically and emotionally safe with your partner?* This is an essential time for you to share your values about them having sex.

Questions and Prompts

- What do you think are good reasons to have sex with someone?
- What are some not-so-good reasons to have sex with someone?
- What are some important things to consider before having sex?
- What are some important things to discuss with your partner before having sex?
- How do you think having sex or not having sex will impact your relationship?

When to have sex for the first time should be a decision every individual gets to make for themselves. Unfortunately, for survivors of sexual abuse, this is not always the case. The best you can do as a parent is to share your values and expectations regarding sexual behaviors, help your child think through all the pros and cons, and provide them with all the information they need to have healthy, pleasurable sexual experiences when they're ready.

Communicating Your Wants and Desires

AGES 16+

In the same way that young people need to learn to say no when it comes to sex, they also need to know that it's important to communicate their wants and desires to a sexual partner without feeling ashamed or embarrassed. Open and honest communication is the key to having pleasurable sexual relationships, but if young people grow up feeling ashamed of their bodies or embarrassed to communicate what feels good to them (or, worse, not knowing what feels good to them), this can become a barrier in future relationships.

Questions and Prompts

♦ Do you think everyone has the same wants or expectations when it comes to sex?

♦ Why do you think some people find sex more pleasurable than others?

♦ Do you think the level of communication between two people affects their sexual relationship?

♦ Do you think a person should tell their sexual partner if something doesn't feel good to them? Why or why not?

♦ Why do you think someone might be embarrassed to tell their sexual partner what feels pleasurable to them?

Don't make this conversation about your child (or about you). Keep it hypothetical and do not overshare when having this (or any other) conversation with your child.

Oral Sex

AGES 13+

Oral sex refers to sexual behaviors such as mouth to vulva, mouth to penis, or mouth to anus. Some young people who are engaging in sexual behaviors with people of another gender may choose to have oral sex to avoid the risk of pregnancy, but all young people need to know that oral sex is not risk-free. STIs, such as chlamydia, gonorrhea, herpes, and the human papillomavirus, can be transmitted through oral sex, and a person can carry these STIs without having any symptoms. It should be noted that the risk of transmitting HIV through oral sex is very low. To reduce the risk of acquiring or transmitting an STI during oral sex, a latex barrier (such as a condom or a dental dam) should be used.

Questions and Prompts

- Do you know what oral sex is?
- How could a person discuss consent before having oral sex?
- Did you know that even though you can't get pregnant from oral sex, certain STIs can be transmitted this way?
- How do you think someone could lower their risk of acquiring an STI if they decide to have oral sex?
- Do you think a lot of young people are having oral sex? Why or why not?
- What are your values/beliefs concerning oral sex?

If a person chooses to engage in mouth-to-vulva or mouth-to-anus sexual behaviors, a latex condom can be used to reduce the risk of STI transmission. By cutting off the tip of the condom, then cutting it from end to end, a flat piece of latex is created that can be laid over the vulva or anus. Remember that this method reduces, but does not eliminate, risk.

Vaginal Sex

AGES 13+

Vaginal sex refers to sexual behaviors that involve inserting something into the vagina (a finger, a penis, a sex toy, etc.) or vulva-to-vulva contact, often referred to as "scissoring." Penile-vaginal sex is the only sexual behavior that can result in a pregnancy. I have encountered many young people over the years who did not receive sex education (or instruction on basic biology) and who didn't know their reproductive system was separate from their digestive system, so they were concerned about pregnancy occurring after having oral sex.

Hormonal contraception can be highly effective in reducing the risk of pregnancy during penile-vaginal sex, but it does not affect the risk of STI transmission. The best way to reduce the risk of both pregnancy and STIs is to use both a hormonal method of contraception and a condom. For people who may experience pain or discomfort during penile-vaginal sex, a water-based lubricant might be helpful in easing the pain and increasing pleasure.

Questions and Prompts

+ Do you know what vaginal sex is?

+ Why do you think it's important to discuss consent before having vaginal sex?

+ How do you think someone could lower their risk of pregnancy or acquiring an STI if they decide to have penile-vaginal sex?

+ Do you know what lubricant is? Why might people use it if they have vaginal sex?

+ Do you think a lot of young people are having penile-vaginal sex? Why or why not?

+ What are your values/beliefs concerning vaginal sex?

If a person chooses to engage in vulva-to-vulva sexual behaviors, a condom can be used to reduce the risk of STI transmission. The tip of the condom can be cut off, then cut from end to end, and the flat piece of latex can be laid between the vulvas. Flavored lubricants should never be used for vaginal sex because they can cause infections.

Anal Sex

AGES 13+

Anal sex refers to sexual behaviors that involve inserting something into the anus (a finger, a penis, a sex toy, etc.) Anyone can engage in anal sex. Young people who are engaging in sexual behaviors may choose to have anal sex to avoid the risk of pregnancy. Like oral sex, anal sex is not risk-free, however, because STIs can be transmitted through anal sex. Since the anus does not naturally lubricate on its own, having anal sex without a water-based lubricant can cause undue pain or harm to the anal tissue. For this reason, unprotected anal sex can be a high-risk behavior for the transmission of HIV and other STIs. To reduce the risk, individuals should use a condom and a water-based lubricant any time they engage in anal sex. Anything that is inserted into the anus (e.g., fingers, sex toys) must be cleaned properly to reduce the risk of potential infection. In addition, any object inserted into the anus should have a flared base to prevent unsafe penetration. If a person has open cuts on their fingers, they should not insert them into someone's anus without using a latex barrier.

Questions and Prompts

+ Do you know what anal sex is?
+ How could a person start a conversation about consent before having anal sex?
+ Did you know that even though you can't get pregnant from anal sex, certain STIs can still be transmitted that way?
+ How do you think someone could lower their risk of acquiring an STI if they decide to have anal sex?
+ Do you know what lubricant is? Why might lubricant be helpful if someone has anal sex?
+ Do you think a lot of young people are having anal sex? What makes you think that?
+ What are your values/beliefs regarding anal sex?

Only water-based lubricant should be used with condoms. Oil-based lubricants, including petroleum jelly (Vaseline), can compromise the latex and cause the condom to break. Some places also sell flavored lubricants, which should never be used for anal or vaginal sex because they can cause infections.

Pleasure

AGES 15+

Not every school-based sex education program discusses pleasure. During conversations about sex, it's important to remember that sex can and should be pleasurable.

Infants and toddlers touch their genitals all the time as a soothing mechanism. It's not sexual behavior at that age, but they know it feels good. Young people have questions about orgasms (what they are and how they feel) and we should be honest in answering these questions. I've actually heard of adults telling young people an orgasm feels like a sneeze. No wonder they are confused! As you engage in these conversations, I encourage you to think about these questions around pleasure: Why is it important for young people to think about what makes them feel good? How can shedding stigma and shame around pleasure have a positive effect on their behavior? If you are part of a culture (ethnic, spiritual, etc.) that believes masturbation is wrong, you should certainly share those values with your child—and I still encourage you to consider these questions.

Questions and Prompts

- Do you discuss sexual pleasure in your sex ed classes?
- Why do you think sex is portrayed as pleasurable in the media, but pleasure isn't mentioned in sex ed?
- Why do you think some people don't talk about pleasure?
- Do you think some people feel ashamed or embarrassed talking about sexual pleasure? If so, why do you think that is?
- What have you heard about orgasms and what they feel like?

Whether through media, hearing peers talk, or in some other way, young people figure out that sex probably feels good. When we don't address pleasure as part of the conversation, young people know we're intentionally leaving something out. This may lead them to wonder what else we're omitting from the discussion—making us, as the adults, a less credible resource. Try to make satisfying curiosity—not increasing it—the goal of your conversations.

Sexual Expectations

AGES 13+

The perfect partner. That special night. Maybe candles are involved? Rose petals? Mood music? This is what TV and the movies might have everyone believe that their first time should be like. If a young person has been exposed to pornography or has experienced any type of sexual abuse, they might also have harmful expectations about what sex is supposed to look and sound like, or how long it's supposed to last. The reality for many people is that the first time they have sex, they're really nervous, it's awkward, it might be painful, and often it's just not the amazing experience Hollywood might have us believe it should be.

I don't suggest that you share with your children the story of your first time (they really don't want to hear that!), but you can, and should, have conversations about the expectations the media may create about sex. You can also emphasize that there's nothing wrong with the individuals or the couple if their experience isn't anything like what they see in the movies.

Questions and Prompts

+ What do you think of the way TV shows and movies portray everyone's first time having sex as being perfect?

+ Do you think most people believe their first time having sex will be like what they see in the movies?

+ What do you think the reality is for most people when they have sex for the first time, as compared to the way it's portrayed in movies?

+ Why do you think most movies don't address how awkward a person's first time having sex can be?

+ Do you think people feel a lot of pressure to make their first time having sex "perfect"? Why do you think they do that?

Many "coming of age" books talk about sexual expectations. Find your favorite and reread it with your child. Then discuss the expectations presented in the book, as compared with what the reality of the situation might look like.

How Pregnancy Happens

AGES 10+

The simple explanation, "When a sperm and an egg get together, they grow into a baby," may be adequate when children are younger, but as they grow up, young people have more questions about pregnancy. Conversations about pregnancy should include an understanding of reproductive anatomy, ovulation and the menstrual cycle, penile-vaginal intercourse, and other ways pregnancies can occur (e.g., in-vitro fertilization, surrogacy), implantation, and the stages of fetal development. It's important to note that, medically, a pregnancy does not occur simply from the joining of the sperm and the ovum, forming a zygote. The zygote may never attach to the uterine lining, and what appears to be a regular period would follow. Pregnancy officially begins after the zygote becomes a blastocyst and attaches to the lining of the uterus. Conversations about pregnancy can naturally flow into discussing prenatal care and birthing types (vaginal birth or cesarean).

Questions and Prompts

- What do you know about pregnancy?
- Do you know how a pregnancy begins?
- Do you know how a person becomes pregnant?
- Did you know that penile-vaginal sex is not the only way a pregnancy can begin?
- Are pregnancy, prenatal care, and birthing types discussed in your sex ed class?

Many different books and websites explain how pregnancy happens in ways that are appropriate for different age groups. A few of my favorites are the books in the series by Robie H. Harris and Michael Emberley (*It's Not the Stork, It's So Amazing!* and *It's Perfectly Normal*) and AMAZE.org, a website for young adolescents (10 to 14 years) and their parents and educators.

Abortion

AGES 13+

Young people should know all the options available in the case of pregnancy. Abortion is a safe and legal option for ending a pregnancy and the vast majority of them are done in the first 12 weeks of pregnancy. Many people have strong feelings about abortion, so talking about your values and beliefs about this topic is important. Two types of abortion are available: a medication abortion and a surgical abortion. A medication abortion involves taking pills prescribed by a doctor that will end a pregnancy. A surgical abortion involves a procedure that uses suction to remove the fetus from the uterus.

Laws governing how old a person needs to be and whether they need a parent's permission to have an abortion vary from state to state. And some states have pursued restrictive laws that make it difficult or even illegal to have an abortion regardless of age. Young people should know about fake clinics called "crisis pregnancy centers." These centers do not actually perform abortions; they exist only to convince people not to have an abortion. Keep in mind that young people benefit from understanding all their options when deciding whether abortion is the right option for them personally.

Questions and Prompts

- Do you know what an abortion is?
- Did you know that there are different types of abortions?
- Why do you think a person might choose to have an abortion?
- How do you think a person might feel when facing the decision about whether to have an abortion?
- Did you know that different states have different laws concerning abortions and minors?
- What are your values/beliefs about abortion?

To get all the facts on abortion, it's best to speak with a clinic that actually provides abortions. To learn more about the abortion laws in your state, visit Guttmacher.org/state-policy/explore/overview -abortion-laws.

Adoption

AGES 13+

In addition to becoming a parent, young people should know all the options available in the case of pregnancy. Adoption is a legal option for people who are not ready and/or able to care for a child at a particular point in their life, but also do not feel that abortion is the right option for them. Adoptions can happen independently, with the support of a lawyer who is familiar with adoption laws, or through a public or private agency. Options are also available pertaining to how much contact the birth parent may choose to have with the child. Open adoptions allow birth parents to know, and have contact with, the adoptive parents and the child. In closed adoptions, there is no contact between the birth parent and the adoptive parents and child once the adoption is final. Laws dealing with adoption vary from state to state, and additional laws exist for international adoptions. Some states also have "safe surrender laws," which allow a person to anonymously surrender an infant at a designated safe haven (e.g., hospitals and fire or police stations) without the risk of legal action. These laws were enacted to save the lives of abandoned newborns.

Questions and Prompts

- Do you know what adoption is?
- Do you know anyone who is adopted?
- Did you know that there are different ways a person can adopt a child or place a child for adoption?
- Have you ever heard of an open or closed adoption?
- What are your values or beliefs concerning adoption?
- Do you know what "safe surrender laws" are?
- Do you know if our state has safe surrender laws?

If you, your child, or someone in your family is adopted, discussing that experience can help personalize the conversation. To learn more about adoption laws in your state, visit ChildWelfare.gov/topics /adoption/laws/laws-state/domestic.

Consent and
Safer Sex

Chapter 6 provides information and prompts to help
you start having sex-positive conversations with the
young people in your life about consent, safer sex
practices, and different forms of sexual violence. It's
important to keep in mind that survivors of child
sexual abuse did not have a choice about remaining
abstinent or deciding when they were ready to have
sex—this will impact the dynamics of all the conversations in this chapter.

What Consent Is

AGES 8+

Consent is informed, voluntary, and mutual agreement
between people to engage in an activity. This can range from
giving a hug or kissing, to engaging in any and all sexual
behaviors. Consent must be given verbally (unless any of
the parties involved has a disability that would prevent
them from verbalizing consent, in which case, another man-
ageable way of giving consent would be required). Young

people also need to know that consent must be given for each sexual behavior—when a person agrees to one sexual behavior, it doesn't mean they agree to *all* sexual behaviors. They also need to understand that consent can be rescinded at *any* time: If they are engaging in a behavior and change their mind, their partner must respect their wishes. A strong understanding of consent derives from a strong sense of bodily autonomy. This is why it's so important for young people to learn that they have control over their bodies. This is a concept that may need to be reestablished for sexual abuse survivors.

Questions and Prompts

+ Do you know what consent is?
+ How would you explain consent?
+ Why is consent important?
+ How would a person ask someone else for their consent?
+ How does a person know if someone else has freely given their consent?
+ What are some things to consider before giving someone consent?
+ What are some ways you would respond if someone does not give their consent?

Modeling bodily autonomy and giving consent is something you can do with a child from the time they are very young. Take every opportunity you have to model asking for, and giving, consent with your child (e.g., "Can I have a hug?" "Can I give you a kiss?"), and respect their response. If you ask for consent and do not respect their response, you're sending the message that when someone has power over you, what the person will power wants is more important than what you want.

What Consent Is Not

AGES 8+

Knowing what consent is *not* is just as important as knowing what consent is. Consent is not a nod, or a shrug, or a look. It needs to be a verbal, freely given yes. If a person says yes, but they are forced or coerced into saying yes, it is not consent (e.g., "If you really cared about me, you would do this"). Consent is not evergreen. If someone consents to a behavior today, it does not mean the other partner automatically has consent to engage in that behavior tomorrow. Consent is not unilateral. All parties involved in a behavior must give consent—not just one of them. Also, consent is not a heterosexual concept. Regardless of the gender(s) or sexual identities of the people engaging in a behavior, *everyone* must give consent.

Questions and Prompts

+ Have you ever seen situations on TV or in the movies where something happened and there was not clear consent? What happened?

+ Can a person give consent through a look or an action? Why or why not?

+ When do you need to ask for a person's consent? Why?

+ What are some ways to let a person know that you do not consent to a behavior?

+ How might you respond if a person is pressuring you or making you feel bad to get you to consent to something?

+ What needs to happen if someone gives consent but then changes their mind?

+ What could happen if a person does not give consent, but the other person does not respect their wishes?

Look for examples of situations on TV or in the movies where there is not clear consent, and use these as an opportunity to ask some of the questions in these sections on consent. When it comes to consent, having young people see what *not* to do is just as important as teaching them what they should do.

Age of Consent

AGES 13+

Age of consent is the legal age at which an individual is considered mature enough to consent to sex. The age of consent varies from state to state, and the specifics of age-of-consent laws for some states may be complicated to understand. Engaging in sex with individuals under the age of consent is considered "statutory rape." In some places, this is true even if both individuals are under the age of consent. Depending on the state, criminal charges based on age-of-consent laws may also be brought in cases of taking and/or transmitting photos or videos of a person who is under the age of consent. It's important for your child to know these laws are in place to protect them from adults with ill intentions. Too often, young people fear getting help when needed if they are in a relationship with, or engaged in behaviors with, someone and one or both parties are under the age of consent (e.g., getting a pregnancy or STI test).

Questions and Prompts

* Do you know what *age of consent* means?
* What do you think the age of consent is in [your state]?
* Why do you think age-of-consent laws exist?
* What do you think age of consent might apply to other than sex?
* How do you think doctors handle age of consent if someone comes in for a pregnancy test or an STI test?

It's important for your child to know they can always come to you to talk about anything. Discussing your values and expectations regarding relationships, sex, and the sharing of sexual photos is critical, but they also need to know they should always come to you, regardless of the situation.

Alcohol, Drugs, and Consent

AGES 14+

When it comes to giving and receiving consent, it is vital for young people to know that a person cannot legally give consent if they are under the influence of alcohol and/or drugs. Since these substances can impair their ability to think clearly, the law prohibits an individual from being able to consent to anything legally while under the influence. This means that if a person says yes while under the influence, it cannot legally be considered consent. Young people need to know that engaging in any kind of sexual behavior while under the influence of alcohol or other drugs is never a good idea.

Questions and Prompts

- What have you learned in school about the effects alcohol or drugs can have on a person?
- How do you think you would respond if someone pressured you to try alcohol or drugs?
- Did you know that a person cannot legally give consent while under the influence of drugs or alcohol? Why do you think that is?
- What do you think could happen if a person gave consent while they were drinking, but later, when they were sober, they realized that they did not want to have sex?

> **The Substance Abuse and Mental Health Services Administration (SAMHSA) recommends talking to your child before they are exposed to alcohol and other drugs, including the misuse of prescription drugs.** In the same way that not talking about sex sends a message, so too does avoiding the topic of alcohol and drugs.

Reproductive Justice

AGES 13+

Reproductive justice is a framework developed by a group of Black women in 1994 out of the need to protect the sexual health rights of women of color, including Indigenous women and transgender people. The framework focuses on three tenets: the right to have or not have children, the right to raise children in safe and sustainable environments, and the right to control their own bodies. This work is typically done through both intersectional and human rights lenses. Many groups focus on reproductive justice, including Sister Song, In Our Own Voice, and the Women of Color Sexual Health Network (WoCSHN).

Questions and Prompts

- Do you know what reproductive justice is?
- Is reproductive justice discussed in your sex ed program?
- Do you know who created the reproductive justice framework?
- Do you know why a group of Black women created the reproductive justice framework?
- Why do you think frameworks like reproductive justice are still necessary today?

External Condoms

AGES 13+

In sex education programs, some states require schools to emphasize the failure rates of condoms instead of noting that using a condom is better than not using any form of protection to reduce the risk of pregnancy and STIs. Young people of all genders need to know how and where to buy condoms (and be aware that there is no minimum age to buy condoms); that condoms come in different sizes and shapes and are made from different materials; and how to use a condom properly. They also need to know that condoms are the only form of contraception that can help reduce—but not completely eliminate—the risk of STIs during oral and anal sex, and both STIs and pregnancy during penile-vaginal sex. Since the testicles are not covered by a condom, STIs transmitted by skin-to-skin contact are still possible. Additionally, remind young people that condoms should never be reused.

Questions and Prompts

♦ Do you know what a condom is?

♦ Why do you think some people use condoms when they have sex?

♦ Do you know that condoms come in different sizes, shapes, and materials? Why do you think so many options exist?

♦ What are some things a person needs to look for when buying condoms?

♦ There are several things you can do to make sure a person is using a condom properly. Do you know what any of them are?

♦ Do you think people of all genders should know where to buy condoms and how to use them? Why or why not?

When you're somewhere that sells condoms, point them out so your child knows exactly where to find them. Explore the various condom brands and the differences between them. Also look at the prices so your child can get a sense of the cost. This should be done with young people of all genders.

Internal Condoms

AGES 13+

Even if your child is receiving sex education in school and is discussing external condoms (previously referred to as "male condoms"), they may not be learning about internal condoms (previously referred to as "female condoms"). The internal condom is inserted into the vagina before sex to help prevent unintended pregnancy, and it also acts as a barrier to reduce the risk of STIs. The only brand of internal condom approved by the FDA is the FC2 internal condom. An internal condom can be used if a sexual partner does not have, or does not want to use, an external condom. This type of condom can be inserted up to two hours before penile-vaginal intercourse and should not be used more than once. An internal condom and an external condom should never be used at the same time because the friction between the two can create heat, which might cause them to break.

Questions and Prompts

- Have you ever heard of an internal condom?
- Did you know that both external and internal condoms are available?
- What do you think the benefits of using an internal condom might be?
- Do you know why internal and external condoms should never be used together?
- Do you know where a person could buy internal condoms?

FC2 internal condoms can be purchased online at FC2.us.com. They are also available in some clinics, such as Planned Parenthood.

Short-Term Contraceptive Options

AGES 12+

Many hormonal options (and a few nonhormonal) options for contraception are available for people who have begun ovulating and menstruating. The pill, the patch, the ring, and the shot are all hormonal options that can reduce the risk of pregnancy for different lengths of time. These methods, which have a high success rate, also allow an individual to have control over how often they get their period. Progesterone-only pills are also available for people who have a sensitivity to estrogen. All of these options require a doctor's prescription, and the shot must be administered by a medical provider. The most common reason contraceptive options fail is they were not used properly (e.g., not taking the pill every day, or forgetting to go back to the doctor's office or clinic after three months for the next shot). Encourage your child to consider their levels of self-efficacy and comfort using their desired option as they make their decision.

Questions and Prompts

- Do you know what contraception is?
- Do you want to start using contraception?
- What types of contraception do you know about? What types of contraception do you want to learn more about?
- What do you think are the pros and cons of [short-term contraceptive option]?
- Do you know how [contraceptive option] works?
- Do you want me to be in the room with you when you talk to the doctor about contraception?
- What questions do you want to ask the doctor about [contraceptive option(s)]?

Hormonal contraception is not just about reducing the risk of pregnancy; it can also regulate menstrual cycles, ease the pain related to premenstrual syndrome (PMS), and reduce acne. Hormonal birth control may have some side effects that your doctor can discuss with you. The choice to begin or end the use of hormones should always be made freely by the individual, including young people with differing abilities.

Long-Term Contraceptive Options

AGES 12+

In addition to the many short-term contraceptive options, longer-term contraceptive options (sometimes referred to as long-acting reversible contraceptives, or LARCs) are also available. The contraceptive implant, sometimes referred to as "the rod," and the intrauterine device (IUD) are both long-term options, since they work for a period of years. Either option must be inserted by a qualified healthcare provider and can be taken out at any time if the person decides they don't like the device or wishes to become pregnant. A nonhormonal IUD option called ParaGard is also available. It uses medical-grade copper to prevent pregnancy for up to 12 years.

Questions and Prompts

+ Do you know what contraception is?

+ What types of contraception do you know about? What types of contraception do you want to learn more about?

+ How do you feel about a healthcare provider having to insert [option] into your body?

+ What do you know about hormonal versus nonhormonal options? What are the pros and cons of each one?

+ What questions do you want to ask the doctor about [contraceptive option(s)]?

It's important to note that there may be a deep distrust of the medical community, especially among BIPOC people, regarding contraceptive options as a result of historical, recent, and present-day reproductive crimes against people of color. If you are fostering a child who is a different race than you, you may want to explore their feelings—and the messages the child has previously received—about contraception.

Emergency Contraception

AGES 13+

Emergency contraception (EC), also known as the morning-after pill, is a medication used to reduce the risk of pregnancy after a person has had sex without protection, or if their contraceptive method failed (e.g., the condom broke, or they realized they'd forgotten to take their pill for the last few days). A brand of EC called Plan B can be purchased by a person of any gender and any age without a prescription. Ella, another brand of EC, requires a prescription from a health-care provider. Plan B must be taken within 72 hours of sex to be effective, and the sooner it is taken, the more effective it is. Ella can be taken up to 120 hours after sex. An IUD can also be used as emergency contraception if it's inserted by a healthcare provider within five days of having sex. EC does not cause abortions (which is a common misconception), and it should only be used in emergency situations, not as a regular method of contraception.

Questions and Prompts

+ Have you ever heard of emergency contraception (EC)?

+ What do you know about EC?

+ Do you know who can purchase EC? Do you think a parent's permission is needed?

+ Why is it important for EC only to be used in emergencies?

+ Where can a person get EC if they need it?

+ Do you know how EC works? If so, how?

+ How long after sex can EC be taken?

When you're somewhere that sells emergency contraception, point it out to your child so they know exactly where they can find it. Also look at the prices, so they can get a sense of the cost. This should be done with young people of all genders.

Sexually Transmitted Infections (STIs)

AGES 13+

The most important things for your child to understand about sexually transmitted infections (STIs) are how they are transmitted, where to get tested, and if and how to be treated. STIs are most commonly transmitted through the transfer of bodily fluids (blood, semen, vaginal fluid, and, in the case of HIV, breast milk) and skin-to-skin contact of the genitals. STIs are not typically transmitted through saliva. People can get tested for STIs in most clinics, including Planned Parenthood. Some STIs can be treated with medications and will go away; others remain in your system for life, and medication can be prescribed to manage the symptoms. One big misconception young people often have is that you can tell if a person has an STI just by looking at them; in fact, the most common "symptom" of STIs is having no symptoms at all. This makes regular testing extremely important.

Questions and Prompts

♦ Do you know what STIs are?

♦ Do you know how a person can acquire or transmit an STI?

♦ What are some ways a person can reduce their risk of acquiring or transmitting an STI?

♦ How can you tell if another person has an STI?

♦ Do you know that some STIs can be cured, and some cannot?

My professional observation is that young people are thinking a lot more about pregnancy than they are about STIs. This would explain why STI rates in the United States are skyrocketing! Remember, you want to keep the conversation positive, even about a subject like STIs. Never talk about people with STIs in a negative way, and do not show your child pictures of genitals with STIs in an attempt to deter them from having sex.

Getting Tested for STIs

AGES 13+

Getting tested for STIs is part of being a sexually healthy adult. Young people need to know why they should get tested, where to get tested, how it happens, and what happens after testing. In most states, a young person can be tested for STIs without parental permission once they reach the age of 13. A big misconception is that there is one test for all the different STIs. The reality is that different tests are required for different STIs. Common STI testing includes a urine test, blood work, an oral swab, and an exam of the genital region. In most cases, the samples obtained are sent to a lab, so results are not available immediately.

If someone tests positive for an STI, they need to notify their recent sexual partners. They may also start a regimen of antibiotics if the STI is bacterial. Young people should be encouraged to be tested and to ask their partner to be tested for STIs before engaging in sexual behaviors so they can take steps to mitigate transmission. Getting tested after engaging in sexual behaviors will only confirm whether they acquired an STI.

Questions and Prompts

- What do you know about STI testing?
- What do you think happens when you get tested for STIs?
- What kinds of tests do you think are used to test for STIs?
- Where do you think people who live near us get tested for STIs?
- What do you think happens after a person gets tested?
- Why is it important to get tested before having sex with a partner?
- What questions should you ask when you make an appointment to get tested?

Reducing shame and stigma around STI testing when talking to young people is important so they feel comfortable getting tested at any time. Sit with your child and model looking up online how to find places near you that offer STI testing. This helps build health literacy skills.

Pre-exposure Prophylaxis (PrEP) and Post-exposure Prophylaxis (PEP)

AGES 15+

Pre-exposure prophylaxis, also known as PrEP, is a daily medication a person can take to reduce their risk of acquiring the human immunodeficiency virus (HIV) before they are exposed to it. PrEP is for people who may have a higher risk of acquiring HIV. While PrEP reduces the risk of acquiring HIV, it does not protect against other STIs. Post-exposure prophylaxis, also known as PEP, is a medication that can be taken up to 72 hours after sex to reduce the risk of acquiring HIV. The sooner PEP is taken after the sexual experience, the more effective it will be. PEP is an option for individuals whose condom broke during sex, those who have had sex without a condom, and those who have experienced rape or sexual assault. Both PrEP and PEP require a prescription from a healthcare provider.

Questions and Prompts

+ What do you know about PrEP and PEP?
+ Do you know why a person might use PrEP or PEP?
+ Do you know when a person should take PrEP or PEP?
+ Do you know where a person would get a prescription for PrEP or PEP?
+ Do you think that PrEP or PEP helps protect against other STIs?

If you see a pharmaceutical commercial to raise awareness about PrEP on TV, that can be a great opportunity to start a conversation about PrEP and PEP.

Gardasil 9 Vaccine

AGES 9+

Gardasil 9 helps protect individuals 9 to 45 years of age against the following diseases caused by nine types of the human papillomavirus (HPV): cervical, vaginal, and vulvar cancers; anal cancer; certain head and neck cancers, such as throat and back-of-mouth cancers; and genital warts. Gardasil 9 is recommended for people of all genders and is administered in two or three shots given in the arm. Although the vaccine can begin to be administered as early as age 9, the CDC (the US Centers for Disease Control and Prevention) recommends beginning the shots at 11 to 12 years of age. Young adults who were not vaccinated at a younger age can still receive the shots up until the age of 26.

Questions and Prompts

- Do you know what vaccines are?
- Why do you think people get vaccines?
- Do you know what HPV is?
- What are some of the complications HPV can cause, and how can you lower those risks?
- What have you heard about Gardasil 9?
- Do you know if any of your friends have had the Gardasil 9 shots? If so, what did they say about it?

Different types of conversations about Gardasil 9 will be appropriate for children at different ages. The questions in this section provide some examples for children on the younger and higher ends of the age range. Your pediatrician should be able to answer any questions you or your child have about Gardasil 9.

Setting Boundaries and Limits

AGES 8+

Modeling and discussing boundaries and limits are the foundation for teaching about consent and thriving relationships as children get older. It's important to discuss setting personal boundaries and how to respect the boundaries of others from an early age. When children are toddlers, parents can begin modeling boundaries and limits by asking their child if they can give them a hug or a kiss, and then respecting the child's response. As young people move through middle school, discussing boundaries related to drugs, alcohol, and sexual behaviors will become essential.

Questions and Prompts

◆ What boundaries and limits have you set/would you like to set related to [insert topic]?

◆ What are some benefits of following through with those boundaries and limits?

◆ What are some potential consequences of not following through with those boundaries and limits?

◆ How would you feel if someone didn't respect the boundaries and limits you set for yourself?

◆ How can you make sure you're respecting other people's boundaries and limits?

◆ What are some ways to show other people that you respect their boundaries and limits?

◆ How do you think someone else would feel if you didn't respect their boundaries and limits?

If your child struggles with setting personal boundaries, you can use the hug example mentioned earlier. Explain what a boundary is, model how the boundary is implemented, and practice the skill together. You might say, "Deciding whether or not you want to give someone a hug is an example of setting a personal boundary. They may ask, 'Can I give you a hug?' And you would reply, 'Sure!' Or maybe, 'Not today.' Personal boundaries work both ways, so you might ask someone if you can give them a hug. Then, no matter how they respond, you must respect their boundaries."

Sexual Harassment

AGES 10+

Sexual harassment includes unwelcome sexual advances, requests for sexual favors, and other verbal or physical harassment of a sexual nature. Sexual harassment can begin as early as middle school, as young people start to experience the physical changes of puberty. Children may think of it as simple teasing—making kissing sounds or faces at others or making comments about their body—but they must learn from an early age that no form of teasing is appropriate, especially teasing of a sexual nature. They may have picked up this behavior from seeing examples on TV or in the movies. It's important to note that these behaviors can happen between people of different genders and people of the same gender.

Questions and Prompts

♦ Do you know what sexual harassment is?

♦ What are some examples of sexual harassment you've seen on TV or in the movies?

♦ Have you ever seen someone being sexually harassed? How do you think it made that person feel?

♦ Do you think it's OK to make comments about someone else's body? Why or why not?

♦ What could you do if you saw someone sexually harassing another person?

When you see examples of sexual harassment on TV and in the movies, point them out. Explain why the behavior is inappropriate and how you feel about it. You can also encourage your child to point out examples when they see them. Ask your child what they would say to the harasser and the person being harassed if they were there.

Sexual Violence and Rape

AGES 12+

One in 9 females and 1 in 53 males under the age of 18 experience sexual abuse or assault at the hands of an adult. Some disabilities may put people at higher risk for crimes like sexual assault or abuse. Rape and other forms of sexual violence are about power and control. (I talked more about this in chapter 4.) Sexual violence may include any number of behaviors, from child sexual abuse, incest, and intimate partner violence to sexual harassment and sexual assault—including unwanted touching, attempted rape, and rape. Teaching about bodily autonomy and consent is an important factor in reducing sexual violence. It's important to believe a person who tells you that they have been sexually assaulted, and they should know it is *never* their fault.

Questions and Prompts

- Why do you think it's important to respect another person's personal boundaries?

- Do you know what it's called if you don't respect another person's boundaries when it comes to sexual behaviors?

- Do you know what sexual violence is? What are some examples you've heard of?

- What are some things you can do if you ever feel unsafe in a situation?

- What are some things you should do if you think the person you're with is feeling unsafe?

- How can you make sure you're not being sexually violent toward someone?

- Sexual violence is *never* the fault of the survivor of the crime. Do you know why?

Research shows that teaching very young children the correct names for their genitals, letting them know who can touch their body, and letting them know who to tell if someone touches their body who should not be touching them are all important factors in child sexual abuse prevention and can be done without raising the child's anxiety levels when it comes to the topic. This is just one of the many reasons that sex education needs to begin at an early age.

Coercion

AGES 13+

Coercion is "the use of express or implied threats of violence or reprisal, or other intimidating behavior, that puts a person in immediate fear of the consequences in order to compel the person to act against their will." Young people need to know that it's never OK to manipulate or pressure a person into doing something they don't want to do. An example of a coercive statement is, "If you really love me, you will [insert behavior] for me." As mentioned earlier in the chapter, if a person is coerced into expressing consent, it is not consent. Coercion is never an acceptable behavior and should be considered a red flag in any relationship—including a friendship, a family relationship, a professional relationship, or a romantic relationship.

Questions and Prompts

- Do you know what *coercion* means?
- Have you ever seen someone try to coerce someone else into doing something they didn't want to do?
- Do you think it's right to try to coerce someone into doing something they don't want to do?
- How do you think it feels for a person who is being coerced?
- How would you respond if a person tried to coerce you into doing something you didn't want to do?

Modeling the behavior you expect of your children is important.
Check your own behavior and the behavior of others in your family, and make sure that coercive statements are not being used to get your child to do things they don't want to do. If you see coercive behavior on TV or in the movies, be sure to point it out, and ask your child how they would respond if someone said something similar to them.

The Internet, Social Media, and Pornography

Technology is ubiquitous in teen culture. Young people have access to more information (and misinformation) in the palm of their hands than any generation before them, so we must talk about the influence of technology when having conversations related to sexuality. Chapter 7 provides some starting points for those conversations.

Online Safety

AGES 8+

When thinking about online safety, the instinct of most parents is to install some sort of parental controls on their children's computer or smartphones. Although this may be helpful during children's younger years, as they get older, they become very skilled at finding ways around parental controls. This is not meant to discourage parents from taking this step, but to remind them that more steps are necessary. Allowing your child to use technology only in shared spaces in the home, permitting a limited amount of time for games/social interaction online, and knowing their passwords are all strategies you can implement to monitor their online activity and keep them safe. Ultimately, we must learn to trust that the young people in our lives will be safe and come to us if something alarming is happening to them. You can build trust through continued conversations with your child, allowing them more freedom with their technology as they get older, and respecting the boundaries you set with them as you increase their privileges.

Questions and Prompts

- What would you do if someone you didn't know tried to talk to you online?
- Why do you think it's important not to share personal information online?
- What are some examples of ways people may share information online without meaning to?
- What are some examples of possible online situations you should tell me about right away?
- Did you know that sometimes people steal another person's profile and try to get information from that person's friends?

If you're concerned about your child's behavior online, try implementing the "hands up" rule. With this rule, if you say, "Hands up," your child must immediately put their hands up without touching any keys or touching the digital device, and allow you to see what is on their screen and in their browsers at that moment. If they do not abide by this, you could implement consequences.

Navigating Social Media

AGES 13+

It's important for you, as a parent, to know the pros and cons of using social media so you can make a fully informed decision around letting your child create accounts. For young people, it can feel like a lot of socializing is happening on these platforms if their peers have accounts. Social media trends may also be the topic of many conversations at school, so some young people may feel pressure to have a social media account. On the flip side, social media is also a place where cyberbullying can occur. Additionally, young people may experience emotional distress if their content doesn't receive positive engagement. Finally, young people often don't realize how much information they're putting out there about themselves when they share content online, which can put them in physical danger.

Questions and Prompts

+ Tell me more about [social media platform].

+ Why do you want to have a [social media] account?

+ Have you thought about the pros and cons of being on [social media]? What are they?

+ What do you think about the possible emotional impact of being on [social media]?

+ What are some safety guidelines we can agree to if you do get a [social media] account?

Most social media platforms do not allow people under the age of 13 to sign up for an account. An example of a safety agreement you might have with your child is that you are connected with their social media account(s) (that is, you're a friend or a follower) and you know their password(s).

Cyberbullying

AGES 8+

Cyberbullying is any type of bullying that can occur out in the real world but is enacted online. Teasing, name-calling, making threats, and intentionally excluding an individual are just some examples of the types of bullying that can happen online. The difference between schoolyard bullying and cyberbullying is that the bullying can be carried into the home and can occur on weekends and holidays if the young person is accessing their technology. For some parents, the instinct may be to take away their child's technology or reduce their access. Although this may remove the threat for your child, they are also being victimized a second time. It's important to teach your child good cyber-citizenship and explain why they should never cyberbully others.

Questions and Prompts

+ Do you know what cyberbullying is?
+ Do you know anyone who has been cyberbullied? If so, what happened?
+ What do you think you should do if someone is cyberbullying you?
+ How do you think it would feel to be cyberbullied?
+ Why do you think it's never OK to cyberbully someone?

If your child experiences cyberbullying, they should stop what they're doing and tell you or another trusted adult what happened. Together, you can then block the person who is doing the bullying. If the bullying is severe and warrants contacting law-enforcement officials, do not delete the interaction; await further instruction from your local authorities.

Discussing Pornography

AGES 13+

With smartphones, young people have access to more information in the palm of their hands than my college library's card catalog contained (of course, not all of it is as reliable). With access to all this information also comes increased access to content that may not be age- or developmentally appropriate, including pornography. According to a 2021 study in the *Journal of Health Communication*, a nationally representative sample of young people in the United States, ages 14 to 18, indicated that 84.4 percent of males and 57 percent of females have been exposed to pornography (Wright et al. 2021). This doesn't necessarily mean that large numbers of young people are seeking out pornography; many of them stumble upon it by accident. Pornography is not a replacement for real sex education, of course, but many young people look to porn to answer their questions when they do not receive sex education.

Questions and Prompts

- Do you know what pornography is?
- Has pornography ever come up when you were looking for something on the internet? If so, what did you do? How did it make you feel?
- Do you understand why pornography is harmful to young people?
- (If your child was actively seeking out pornography) What were you trying to find out by looking at pornography?
- What questions do you have about sex or people's bodies?

If you find out your child has been exposed to pornography, the most important thing you can do is stay calm. Start the conversation by asking questions and find out how they came across it. If they stumbled upon it, find out how they reacted when they saw it and how they're feeling about it. Then take the opportunity to explain why pornography is not developmentally appropriate for young people.

Sexting

AGES 13+

Sexting is the practice of sending nude or partially nude pictures or videos to another person. For young people, sexting (or sending nudes) is often a way of exploring their sexuality with another person. A recent study showed about one in seven of those between the ages of 12 and 17 had sent sexts (Madigan et al. 2018). The big problem with sexting is that, by law, pictures of naked minors are considered child pornography and thus are illegal. Different states handle issues of creating and distributing child pornography differently, but it's important for young people to understand this legal issue. Young people should also be prompted to think about what might happen if their pictures were shared with other people they were not intended for or if they showed up online somewhere.

Questions and Prompts

- Do you know what sexting is?
- Do you think sexting is a problem? Why or why not?
- How do you think law-enforcement officials handle sexting cases?
- Do you think there's a chance that other people might see the pictures that were sent privately?
- How do you think someone would feel if their private pictures were shared with others without their permission?

Building trust when it comes to technology is important, and enforcing consequences when trust is broken is equally important. Have conversations about responsible phone use before your child gets a smartphone. It's a good idea to set parameters for when and how the phone will be used when your child firsts get it. Some parents and caregivers may even choose to keep the phone with them each night, especially with younger adolescents.

Sex Trafficking

AGES 12+

Sex trafficking is "the action or practice of illegally transporting people from one country or area to another for the purpose of sexual exploitation." Traffickers often use coercive tactics on vulnerable individuals to lure them into illegal commercial sex acts. A large number of child sex trafficking survivors in the United States entered the sex trade once they were in the foster care system, with the average age between 12 and 14. Traffickers find victims of all genders through the internet and social media networks and promise them things such as love, money, and protection in exchange for prostitution, appearing in pornography, and other sexual behaviors.

Questions and Prompts

- Have you ever heard of human trafficking or sex trafficking?
- What do you know about human trafficking or sex trafficking?
- How do you think traffickers find young people?
- How might traffickers try to convince young people to participate in sexual behaviors?
- What are some signs that a person is trying to traffic someone? What should you look out for?
- What should you do if a person starts asking you sexual questions or promises you things in exchange for sexual behaviors?

It is essential for you to discuss with the young people in your life the tactics that traffickers use to lure children into trafficking. Make an agreement with your child that if a person they don't know reaches out to them online, they will let you know immediately. To contact the National Human Trafficking Hotline, call 1-888-373-7888 or text 233733.

A Final Word

Congratulations on completing this book and taking an important step toward having conversations with your child about sexuality that can be lifesaving and affirming. Hopefully, you now feel better prepared with the facts than you did before you started reading, and you've picked up some tips for making your conversations successful. You may be feeling a bit overwhelmed by the number of topics and conversations in this book. If so, take a deep breath, and remember that these conversations will take place over several years. As I mentioned in the introduction, talking about sexuality is a lifelong conversation.

While some of these conversations may stretch you beyond your comfort zone, I assure you that achieving the goals of sex education mentioned in the introduction to part 2 are well worth the discomfort. A vocal minority may try to convince you that talking about sexuality is immoral and is stealing your child's innocence. The fact is, talking about all the topics covered in this book in developmentally appropriate ways will not only help inform and protect your child, but also prepare them to be adults who are sexually healthy and happy in their relationships—and who doesn't want that for the young people they love?

Resources

Websites

GenderSpectrum.org
Gender Spectrum works to create gender-sensitive and inclusive environments for all children and teens. The site contains resources for youth and other family members on understanding gender, as well as information on medical, mental health, and social service resources, and more.

PFLAG.org
PFLAG, the first and largest organization for lesbian, gay, bisexual, transgender, and queer (LGBTQ+) people and their parents, families, and allies, has more than 400 chapters across the country. It provides confidential peer support, education, and advocacy for LGBTQ+ people and their families and allies in all 50 states.

PlannedParenthood.org
Planned Parenthood provides a large range of healthcare services, including pregnancy and STI testing, contraception, abortions, mammograms, and LGBTQ health services. Services vary based on location.

SexEtc.org
Sex, Etc. is a product of Answer, a national sex education organization based at Rutgers University. It produces age-appropriate and medically accurate sexual health content, written by and for high school–age teens.

SisterSong.net
Sister Song is a women of color reproductive justice collective. This organization works to improve institutional policies and systems that impact the reproductive lives of marginalized communities through a reproductive justice lens.

Hotline Numbers

LGBT National Hotline
Call 888-843-4564

National Domestic Violence Hotline
Call 800-799-SAFE (7233)
Text "start" to 88788

National Human Trafficking Hotline
Call 1-888-373-7888
Text 233733

National Sexual Assault Hotline
Call 800-656-4673

Trevor Lifeline
Call 866-488-7386

Podcasts

NPR: A Sex Ed Update for an Internet-Enabled Generation
NPR.org/2020/02/26/809741258/a-sex-ed-update-for-an-internet
-enabled-generation
NPR's Ailsa Chang talks with Cory Turner and Anya Kamenetz,
fellow NPR contributors, who share findings from their conversations with various sex educators they've interviewed for their *Life
Kit* podcast.

**NPR: For Some with Intellectual Disabilities, Ending Abuse
Starts with Sex Ed**
NPR.org/2018/01/09/572929725/for-some-with-intellectual
-disabilities-ending-abuse-starts-with-sex-ed
NPR's Joseph Shapiro shares the findings of an NPR investigation
into sexual abuse against people with intellectual disabilities and
the importance of sex education for this population.

References

"2019 Trafficking in Persons Report - State." Accessed September 14, 2021. https://www.state.gov/wp-content/uploads/2019/06 /2019-TIP-Introduction-Section-FINAL.pdf.

"Abortion Care." ACOG. Accessed September 14, 2021. https://www .acog.org/womens-health/faqs/induced-abortion.

Arain, Mariam, Maliha Haque, Lina Johal, Puja Mathur, Wynand Nel, Afsha Rais, Ranbir Sandhu, and Sushil Sharma. "Maturation of the Adolescent Brain." *Neuropsychiatric Disease and Treatment* (2013): 449. doi.org/10.2147/ndt.s39776.

Blogkaya. "The Facts on Tampons-and How to Use Them Safely: FDA." September 14, 2021. https://business.aseandestination .com/host-https-www.fda.gov/consumers/consumer-updates /facts-tampons-and-how-use-them-safely.

Cass, Vivienne C. "Homosexual Identity Formation." *Journal of Homosexuality* 4, no. 3 (1979): 219–235. doi.org/10.1300 /j082v04n03_01.

Coaston, Jane. "The Intersectionality Wars." Vox. Vox, May 20, 2019. https://www.vox.com/the-highlight/2019/5/20/18542843 /intersectionality-conservatism-law-race-gender-discrimination.

"Coercion." Merriam-Webster. Merriam-Webster. Accessed September 14, 2021. https://www.merriam-webster.com /dictionary/coercion.

Crenshaw Kimberlé. *On Intersectionality: Essential Writings.* New York: The New Press, 2017.

"Emotional Development." Be You. Accessed September 14, 2021. https://beyou.edu.au/fact-sheets/social-and-emotional-learning /emotional-development.

Fang, Janet. "The Deadly Consequences of Hypersexualizing Asian Women." Scientific American, April 19, 2021. https://www.scientificamerican.com/article/the-deadly-consequences-of-hypersexualizing-asian-women/.

"FC2® Internal Condom: The Female Health Company." FC2 Female Condom, July 7, 2021. https://fc2.us.com/.

Finkelhor, David, Anne Shattuck, Heather A. Turner, and Sherry L. Hamby. "The Lifetime Prevalence of Child Sexual Abuse and Sexual Assault Assessed in Late Adolescence." *Journal of Adolescent Health* 55, no. 3 (2014): 329–333. doi.org/10.1016/j.jadohealth.2013.12.026.

Future of Sex Education Initiative. *National Sex Education Standards: Core Content and Skills, K–12,* 2nd ed. (2020). AdvocatesForYouth.org/wp-content/uploads/2021/08/NSES-2020-web-updated.pdf.

"Girlhood Interrupted - Georgetown Law." Accessed September 14, 2021. https://www.law.georgetown.edu/poverty-inequality-center/wp-content/uploads/sites/14/2017/08/girlhood-interrupted.pdf.

Goldfarb, Eva S., and Lisa D. Lieberman. "Three Decades of Research: The Case for Comprehensive Sex Education." *Journal of Adolescent Health* 68, no. 1 (2021): 13–27. doi.org/10.1016/j.jadohealth.2020.07.036.

"Help Protect Your Child Today from Certain HPV-Related Cancers Later in Life with Gardasil 9." HPV Vaccine Information for Parents of Boys and Girls. Accessed September 14, 2021. https://www.gardasil9.com/adolescent/.

Holland-Hall, Cynthia, and Elisabeth H. Quint. "Sexuality and Disability in Adolescents." *Pediatric Clinics of North America* 64, no. 2 (2017): 435–449. doi.org/10.1016/j.pcl.2016.11.011.

"How Common Is Intersex?" Intersex Society of North America. Accessed September 14, 2021. https://isna.org/faq/frequency/.

"Human Trafficking into and within the United States: A Review of the Literature." ASPE. Accessed September 14, 2021. https://aspe.hhs.gov/reports/human-trafficking-within-united-states-review-literature-0#Trafficking.

"'I Want to Be like Nature Made Me.'" Human Rights Watch, December 15, 2020. https://www.hrw.org/report/2017/07/25/i-want-be-nature-made-me/medically-unnecessary-surgeries-intersex-children-us.

Kantor, Leslie, and Nicole Levitz. "Parents' Views on Sex Education in Schools: How Much Do Democrats and Republicans Agree?" *PLOS ONE* 12, no. 7 (2017). doi.org/10.1371/journal.pone.0180250.

Kreager, Derek A., and Jeremy Staff. "The Sexual Double Standard and Adolescent Peer Acceptance." *Social Psychology Quarterly* 72, no. 2 (2009): 143–164. doi.org/10.1177/019027250907200205.

Madigan, Sheri, Anh Ly, Christina L. Rash, Joris Van Ouytsel, and Jeff R. Temple. "Prevalence of Multiple Forms of Sexting Behavior among Youth." *JAMA Pediatrics* 172, no. 4 (2018): 327–335. doi.org/10.1001/jamapediatrics.2017.5314.

"Medical Abortion." Mayo Clinic. Mayo Foundation for Medical Education and Research, May 14, 2020. https://www.mayoclinic.org/tests-procedures/medical-abortion/about/pac-20394687.

"Misogyny." Merriam-Webster. Merriam-Webster. Accessed September 14, 2021. https://www.merriam-webster.com/dictionary/misogyny.

"Physical Development in Boys: What to Expect." HealthyChildren.org. Accessed September 14, 2021. https://www.healthychildren.org/English/ages-stages/gradeschool/puberty/Pages/Physical-Development-Boys-What-to-Expect.aspx.

"Physical Development in Girls: What to Expect during Puberty."
HealthyChildren.org. Accessed September 14, 2021. https://
www.healthychildren.org/English/ages-stages/gradeschool
/puberty/Pages/Physical-Development-Girls-What-to-Expect
.aspx.

Parenthood, Planned. "What Are Puberty Blockers?" Planned
Parenthood. Accessed September 14, 2021. https://www
.plannedparenthood.org/learn/teens/puberty/what-are
-puberty-blockers.

"Pregnancy Week by Week Healthy Pregnancy." Mayo Clinic. Mayo
Foundation for Medical Education and Research, November 13,
2020. https://www.mayoclinic.org/healthy-lifestyle/pregnancy
-week-by-week/basics/healthy-pregnancy/hlv-20049471.

"Puberty Blockers." Hormone Blockers | St. Louis Childrens Hospital.
Accessed September 14, 2021. https://www.stlouischildrens.org
/conditions-treatments/transgender-center/puberty-blockers.

"Rape Culture." Womens Gender Center. Accessed September 14,
2021. https://www.marshall.edu/wcenter/sexual-assault/rape
-culture/.

"Reproductive Justice." Sister Song. Accessed September 14, 2021.
https://www.sistersong.net/reproductive-justice.

"Risk and Protective Factors|sexual Violence|violence Prevention|
injury Center|CDC." Centers for Disease Control and Prevention,
February 5, 2021. https://www.cdc.gov/violenceprevention
/sexualviolence/riskprotectivefactors.html.

Salovey, Peter, and John D. Mayer. "Emotional Intelligence." *Imagi-
nation, Cognition and Personality* 9, no. 3 (1990): 185–211.
doi.org/10.2190/dugg-p24e-52wk-6cdg.

"Sexual Harassment." RAINN. Accessed September 14, 2021.
https://www.rainn.org/articles/sexual-harassment.

Spencer, Jennifer M., Gregory D. Zimet, Matthew C. Aalsma, and Donald P. Orr. "Self-Esteem as a Predictor of Initiation of Coitus in Early Adolescents." *PEDIATRICS* 109, no. 4 (2002): 581–584. doi.org/10.1542/peds.109.4.581.

Squeglia, Lindsay M., and Kevin M. Gray. "Alcohol and Drug Use and the Developing Brain." *Current Psychiatry Reports* 18, no. 5 (2016). doi.org/10.1007/s11920-016-0689-y.

"Stanford Children's Health." Cognitive Development in Adolescence. Accessed September 14, 2021. https://www .stanfordchildrens.org/en/topic/default?id=cognitive -development-90-P01594.

"State Legislation Tracker." Guttmacher Institute, November 1, 2021. https://www.guttmacher.org/state-policy/explore/sex -and-hiv-education and https://www.guttmacher.org/state -policy/explore/overview-abortion-laws.

Tajfel, H., and J. C. Turner. "An Integrative Theory of Inter-Group Conflict." In W. G. Austin and S. Worchel, eds., *The Social Psychology of Inter-Group Relations* (pp. 33–47). Monterey, CA: Brooks/Cole, 1979.

"The Growing Child: Adolescent 13 to 18 Years." Johns Hopkins Medicine. Accessed September 14, 2021. https://www .hopkinsmedicine.org/health/wellness-and-prevention /the-growing-child-adolescent-13-to-18-years.

"United States Age of Consent Map." United States Age of Consent Laws By State. Accessed September 14, 2021. https://www .ageofconsent.net/states.

"Why You Should Talk with Your Child about Alcohol and Other Drugs." SAMHSA. Accessed September 14, 2021. https://www .samhsa.gov/talk-they-hear-you/parent-resources/why-you -should-talk-your-child.

"Women's Marital Status - Census.gov." Accessed September 14, 2021. https://www.census.gov/content/dam/Census/library /visualizations/time-series/demo/families-and-households /ms-1b.pdf.

Wright, Paul J., Bryant Paul, and Debby Herbenick. "Preliminary Insights from a U.S. Probability Sample on Adolescents' Pornography Exposure, Media Psychology, and Sexual Aggression." *Journal of Health Communication* 26, no. 1 (2021): 39–46. doi.org/10.1080/10810730.2021.1887980.

"Your First Period." ACOG. Accessed September 14, 2021. https://www.acog.org/womens-health/faqs/your-first-period.

"Your Menstrual Cycle." Your menstrual cycle | Office on Women's Health. Accessed September 14, 2021. https://www .womenshealth.gov/menstrual-cycle/your-menstrual-cycle.

Index

A

Abortion, 87–88
Abstinence, 72–73
Abstract thinking, vs concrete, 8
Abuse, recognizing, 68–69. *See also*
    Equitable relationships;
    Sexual violence and rape
Adolescence, 3
Adoption, 88–89
Affection, showing, 59–60
Alcohol, drugs, and consent, 94–95
Alcohol, effects of, 7
Anal sex, 82–83
Asexual, 12
Assigned female at birth (AFAB),
    physical changes in, 4–5
Assigned male at birth (AMAB),
    physical changes in, 5, 7

B

Beliefs. *See* Values and beliefs
Bodily autonomy, 91
Body image, 14, 39–40
Body odor, 4, 36–37
Boundaries and limits, setting, 106–107

C

Changes, normalizing, 30–31
Cisgender, 6
Coercion, 110–111
Cognitive development, 7
Coming out, 45–46
Communicating wants and
    desires, 79–80
Communication in relationships,
    58–59

Concrete vs abstract thinking, 8
Condoms, 83, 96–98
Conflict resolution, 55–56
Consent
    age of, 93–94
    under the influence of alcohol
        and drugs, 94–95
    what it is, 90–91
    what it is not, 92–93
Contraception
    emergency, 101–102
    long-term options, 100
    short-term options, 98–99
Contraceptive implant, 100
Crenshaw, Kimberlé, 44
Cyberbullying, 115

D

Dennis Dailey, Dr., vi
Douching, 38
Drugs, effects of, 7. *See also* Alcohol,
    drugs, and consent

E

Emergency contraception, 101–102
Emotional development, 7–8
Emotional intelligence, 41–42
Emotional intimacy, 57–58
Ending a relationship, 65–66.
    See also Rejection
Equitable relationships, 61–62

F

Fielding questions, 24–26
First love, 54–55

G

Gardasil 9 vaccine, 105–106
Gender expression, 6, 51–52
Gender identity, 6, 45–46, 48–49
Guided conversations, about, ix

H

Holistic sexuality, vi
Hooking up, 64–65
Hormonal contraception, 81, 98–99
Hormone-blocking therapies, 6.
    See also Puberty blockers
Hypersexualization, 44

I

Independence, striving for, 10
Infections. See Sexually transmitted
    infections (STIs)
Influence of peers,16
Initiating conversations, 21, 23–24
Intersecting identities, 44–45
Intersectionality, 44
Intersex variations, 52–53
Intimacy. See Emotional intimacy
Intrauterine device (IUD), 100

J

Jealousy, 60–61

K

Knowing when you're ready, 77–78

L

Lev, Arlene Istar, 48

M

Marijuana, effects of, 7
Masturbation, 35–36.
    See also Pleasure

Menstrual cups. See Pads, tampons,
    and menstrual cups
Menstruation, 31–32
Modern technology, impact of, 11
Mood swings, 9–10
Morning-after pill, 101

N

Negotiation, 67–68
Nocturnal emissions, 7, 34–35
Nude pictures. See Sexting

O

Online safety, 112–113
Oral sex, 80
Orgasms. See Pleasure

P

Pads, tampons, and menstrual
    cups, 33–34
Peer pressure, handling 75–76.
    See also Influence of peers
Period. See Menstruation
Period products. See Pads, tampons,
    and menstrual cups
Physical changes
  in people assigned female
      at birth (AFAB), 4–5
  in people assigned male at
      birth (AMAB), 5, 7
  normalizing, 30–31
Pill, the, 98–99
Plan B, 101
Pleasure, 83–84
Pornography, discussing, 116–117
Post-exposure prophylaxis
      (PEP), 104–105
Power dynamics in relationships,
      63–64
Pre-exposure prohylaxis
      (PrEP), 104–105

Prefrontal cortex (PFC), 8–9
Pregnancy
   abortion, 87–88
   adoption, 88–89
   condoms, 83, 96–98
   emergency contraception, 101–102
   how it happens, 86–87
   long-term contraceptive
      options, 100
   short-term contraceptive
      options, 98–99
   vaginal sex, 81–82
Premenstral syndrome (PMS), 32
Privacy, a growing desire for, 13
Puberty, 3–5, 7
Puberty blockers, 49–50

Q

Questions, fielding, 24–26

R

Rape. *See* Sexual violence and rape
Recognizing abuse, 68–69
Rejection, 66–67
Relationships
   communication, 58–59
   ending, 65–66
   equitable, 61–62
   power dynamics, 63–64
   rejection, 66–67
Reporting sexual assault, 70–71
Reproductive justice, 95–96
Rod, the, 100
Romantic feelings, 10, 12

S

Safety
   cyberbullying, 115
   navigating social media, 114
   online, 112–113

sexting, 117
Self-care, hygiene and, 36–37
Self-esteem, 14, 40–41
Semen, 7, 34
Sex assigned at birth, 6
Sex education in schools, 19
Sex-positive talks,
   importance of, 17–19
Sexting, 117–118
Sex trafficking, 118–119
Sexual abuse. *See* Sexual
   violence and rape
Sexual assault, reporting, 70–71.
   See also Sexual violence and rape
Sexual behavior. *See specific*
Sexual curiosity, affirming, 73–74
Sexual development, a primer on, 3
Sexual expectations, 85–86
Sexual harassment, 108
Sexual identity, 15–16, 44, 47–48
Sexually transmitted infections
   (STIs), 102–103
   anal sex, 82–83
   condoms, 96–98
   Gardasil 9 vaccine, 105–106
   getting tested for, 103–104
   oral sex, 80
   post-exposure prophylaxis
      (PEP), 104–105
   pre-exposure prophylaxis
      (PrEP), 104–105
   vaginal sex, 81–82
Sexual orientation, 15–16.
   See also Coming out
Sexual violence and rape, 109–110
Social acceptance. *See*
   Influence of peers
Social development, 12–16
Social groups, changing, 42–43
Social identity theory, 43

Social media, navigating, 114
SOW method, 15
Spontaneous erections and
    wet dreams, 34–35
Statutory rape, 93

T

"The talk." *See* Initiating conversations
Tampons. *See* Pads, tampons,
    and menstrual cups
Technology, impact of, 11
Transgender, 6
Transgender emergence model, 48

V

Vaginal sex, 81–82
Values and beliefs, 14–15, 22
    defining, 26–27
    SOW method, 15
Violence. *See* Coercion; Equitable
        relationships; Sexual
        violence and rape
Virginity, the construct of, 76–77

W

Wants and desires, communicating, 79
Wet dreams, spontaneous
        erections and, 34–35

Acknowledgments

I want to start by thanking my family and friends for all their love and support. There are too many of you to mention individually, but you know who you are. Thank you for always believing in me.

I also want to thank all my incredible sex education mentors—especially Nora Gelperin, Elizabeth Schroeder, and Eva Goldfarb, my first mentors—who taught me so much of the information shared in this book.

Finally, I want to thank Matt Buonaguro at Callisto Media and Brian Sweeting and everyone at Rockridge Press who helped make this book possible. Thank you for entrusting me with this project.

About the Author

As a leader in the field of sex education, **Daniel Rice, MEd,** contributed to the writing of *National Sex Education Standards*, second edition, and cochaired the committee that developed the Professional Learning Standards for Sex Education. In addition to his work expanding national access to sex education, Rice has extensive experience working directly with youth in public and private schools, community-based organizations, foster programs, the juvenile justice system, communities of faith, teen-to-teen leadership programs, and mentoring groups. Rice's expertise in sex education has led him to be a guest on NPR and he has been quoted in the *New York Times*, the *Los Angeles Times*, the *Chicago Tribune*, and *Rewire News Group*. He holds a master of education degree in curriculum and instruction from Western New England University and a bachelor's degree in psychology from Wagner College.

CPSIA information can be obtained
at www.ICGtesting.com
Printed in the USA
JSHW042030200222
23143JS00001B/1

9 781638 074229